ALL IN A DAY'S WORK

Previous Publications

Diet for the Soul

Divine Healing – Resources and Limitations

Healing and the Mind of Christ

Towards Health and Wholeness

Moments Remembered

◆

First published 1997

Published by Andrew P. McComb

Typeset by December Publications

Printed by the Universities Press (Belfast) Ltd

*Front cover by Ulster Artist, Colin Corkey –
based on garden at Ivy Cottage, Author's Home*

ALL IN A DAY'S WORK

ANDREW P. McCOMB

FOREWORD

In recent years a great number of books has been written about Divine Healing, many of them the result of much thought and wide experience. I have no intention of adding to that list but it has been suggested that it might be helpful to some people if I were to share a few of my experiences in this healing ministry so dear to the heart of our Lord. I have gladly done that in this little volume and in such a way as to suggest that the ministry of Divine Healing is not just an addendum, something added on to pastoral ministry, but rather that it is an integral part of total ministry. So the 'experiences' are deliberately mixed up for that is how it often is in ministerial life, e.g. one might be presiding at a meeting of Kirk Session, perhaps discussing a topic like the attendance at the Sunday evening service and later ministering to someone who has just been told he is suffering from cancer. It is a great joy to know that this type of ministry to the whole person is growing in our church and it is my hope and prayer that this collection of 'experiences' may help towards this end.

My sincere thanks to those who have made it all possible; to my wife Queenie, who has not only read through these 'experiences' but who has lived through many of them and has ever been a tower of strength; to Aline Hanna who must bear responsibility for launching me in the sphere of writing, but having done so, gallantly undertook to interpret my handwriting and word-process the manuscript; to Brenda Berner whose mastery of the English language and meticulous proof-reading ensured a more polished and accurate end-product; and lastly my thanks to my enthusiastic band of book-sellers who tell me they are a-rarin' to go!

The entire proceeds will be donated to the Chest, Heart and Stroke Association.

Andrew P. McComb

The Author's home Church, Loanends, on the Seven Mile Straight.
A fine suite of halls has been added in recent years, to right of photo.

CONTENTS

1

A Belated Start

If you read the annals of Scottish congregations, from time to time you will come across the term 'stikit minister'. This was applied to students for the ministry who had fulfilled all necessary requirements, academic and spiritual, but who for some reason never proceeded to ordination. The term was seldom used in the Presbyterian Church here, although from time to time there were some to whom it might have been applied. I can think of two such people. One had difficulty in subscribing to the Westminster Confession of Faith, a must for those entering the ministry of the Presbyterian Church. To withdraw meant a great sacrifice but he was an honest man and for him there was no other way. He had a good brain and kept up his reading in many different spheres as well as running the home farm, so he must have finished up a very well educated farmer! The other was a young man as was said 'of nervous disposition' who found it hard to speak to an audience. He was, however, gifted musically and had a very happy and successful career in music.

Now I was not in danger of becoming a 'stikit minister' but I hesitated quite a long time before deciding to conduct a service of worship. It wasn't lack of confidence but rather a sense of unworthiness. The thought of leading people into God's presence and speaking to Him on their behalf and then in preaching, to bring them a word from the Lord, was something which I found really awesome. To be honest this is a feeling I have never quite lost and some would say that this is how it should be.

However, I had a friend, James McBride, who understood this but felt that the time for me to make a start had arrived. On a certain Sunday he had been invited to 'supply' a charge in which there were two congregations, a large one and a much smaller one. His suggestion was that I would be responsible for the smaller service. Well, that was an offer that one could not turn down and so on the appointed Sunday morning we set off for the country, I wearing a clerical collar for the first time!

I sat in the pew for the first service when my friend preached an excellent

Staff and Students at Assembly's College, 1940–1941.

sermon and conducted prayer and readings in a very inspiring manner, but I have to admit that my thoughts tended to stray to the service that was to follow! Here the order was reversed, my friend went to the pew while I was taken to what was called the session house. I was received by an elder with a long white beard. I warned him that this was my first attempt at conducting a service and not to expect too much. He was very considerate, offering a helpful prayer before we left to walk to the church. It was a quaint little building and as I walked up the aisle I had to pass a large coal heater which I was told kept the congregation comfortable in the coldest days of winter, especially if the sexton got the fire lighted early enough!

The service seemed to go quite well, certainly better than I had dared to imagine, although I knew that as well as the old elder, others at home were remembering me in prayer. I was keenly aware of the presence of the Lord and my apprehension faded away as I spoke to Him in prayer and brought His Word to the people.

The old Church at Kilkinamurry in which the author conducted his first Service.

After the service I returned to the session house where my old friend, the elder, was waiting for me. 'Man dear,' he said as he shook me by the hand, 'in two or three years time you'll be worth hearin'.'

I'm not sure if his forecast was fulfilled or not, but I felt that he spoke with real appreciation and encouragement and with a gentle suggestion that I had a bit to go! How we all in both pulpit and pew need that little reminder. Jesus said that we were to seek perfection – we all have a bit to go!

My friend, James McBride, spent his ministry in Duneane and First Randalstown and tragically passed away some twenty years ago, the result of a brain tumour. I shall never forget the kindness and thoughtfulness which he showed as he launched me on my preaching career.

The little church in Kilkinamurry has long since disappeared – I thought that in view of that eventful Sunday morning it might have been 'listed'! Not so however; it was found to be in a dangerous condition and replaced by a beautiful new building in 1955.

2

Unforgettable

As we travel the way of life we meet all kinds of people, many of whom are as ships that pass in the night; they are soon forgotten, perhaps because most people, including ourselves, are just ordinary, normal beings. However, from time to time someone crosses our path who is different and who for some reason makes an indelible impression on our minds. Such a one was the Clerk of Session in my first congregation, Sam Ferguson of Killycopple. Sam had spent a good part of his life in a solicitor's office and was thus qualified to give a little legal advice to his neighbours, especially when it came to making wills. He never accepted any gratuity for his services, as money was certainly not at the top of his list of priorities.

Eventually he had to leave the office and come home to look after an invalid sister and his small farm. He was qualified for neither task. He used to tell me that he was good at boiling an egg but that was about the extent of his cooking! And as regards the livestock on the farm, his main concern was that they should be well fed and comfortable rather than that they should make a living for their owner!

I remember my first visit to his home. I couldn't see anyone but I could hear a voice and assumed that he was having a chat with a neighbour, so I followed the sound and found Sam talking, not to a neighbour, but to his small flock of hens. As far as I could see, not only the rooster but every hen had a name and he knew each one 'personally!' A story went the rounds that one day he caught a rat in a cage trap – the average farmer would quickly have bumped it off, but not so Sam. He is supposed to have taken it to the far side of the meadow and before releasing it, to have given this warning, 'Now boy, let this be a lesson to you, don't come back again!'

With this love for God's creatures went a great love for the Lord Himself. In the book of Genesis we learn about Enoch; not much is said about him apart from the fact that he was the father of Methuselah, and the wonderful tribute that 'he walked with God'. I think that this could have been said about Sam – to be in his presence made you feel that here was someone to whom God was wonderfully real and on whose life the Spirit had a powerful influence.

This came out very clearly when he led in prayer either in Kirk Session or Sunday School. As he took the opening prayer, I can recall words like these, 'Lord we thank You for this fine morning, a wee bit cold but nice all the same.' It went on in this manner and when he finished and we opened our eyes, we almost felt that God was standing beside him!

There was a problem here, however, as Sam's prayers sometimes became so real and meaningful that he completely forgot about time! On one occasion when we were having a special service with a guest preacher, this failing rather upset things. The service was due to start at 7.00 pm and Sam's task was to receive the visiting minister, showing him to the vestry. A few minutes before time, the visitor invited Sam to seek God's blessing upon the service in a short prayer. Well, that would normally be a proper thing to do, but not so in this case, for Sam went on and on in his prayer while the large congregation waited and the guest preacher sweated! After some minutes he had to call a halt for Sam was quite oblivious of the passing of time!

But while he seemed to live up in the clouds his feet were firmly on the ground as the following little episode will show. At this particular time we had decided to build a church hall and as money was really scarce, I knew that my job would be to push the scheme as hard as I could. We asked our members to promise an amount to be paid over three years. So having made a very strong appeal, I felt that I must, using a modern phrase, put my money where my mouth was and make a fairly generous promise. Now somehow Sam heard about this and came to me to discuss the matter, telling me that I shouldn't have promised so much. When I asked him why, his reply was that I would probably move after a few years and I and my family would not receive the enjoyment and benefit from the proposed hall that would accrue to the members of the congregation. I admitted that he had got a point but that my reward would be to see the hall playing an important part in the building-up of the Kingdom especially amongst our young people. Sam wasn't altogether satisfied with this and as he went off he simply said with a touch of his legal training, 'I will certainly keep the matter in mind.' Some years later Sam passed away and in his will left me exactly double the amount I had promised for the hall – that is how he 'kept the matter in mind'!

As far as I can remember Sam had never been to Belfast and as our wedding day came along, he was sent an invitation, although I wasn't hopeful that he would accept. However, he called at the manse to thank me for the invitation and then, typical of his honesty, he asked me a searching question. 'Have you invited me because I am Clerk of Session or do you really want me to come?' I replied with equal frankness that if I hadn't wanted him to come he would not have been invited! 'Then I'll be there,' was his quick reply.

The wedding reception was held in the Grand Central Hotel, Belfast, long since disappeared, and after the meal there was the usual round of speeches including Sam's. In simple but well chosen words he welcomed the bride who would be coming as the lady of Redrock manse, assuring her of the love and support of the people. After his death his nephew very kindly passed on to me some of his letters and articles, including a copy of this speech which I still possess and greatly cherish. It was a delightful effort and when he sat down he got a hearty round of applause for he had won the hearts of all present. My last glimpse of Sam that day occurred as we drove away from the hotel after the reception. He was walking along Royal Avenue, his thumbs in the armholes of his waistcoat, looking up at the high buildings, obviously impressed by all he saw! I never learnt how he got home but he eventually made it for on our return from honeymoon, we were barely into the manse when Sam arrived to welcome us – what a friend!

Sam loved to whistle, today almost a lost art, and when he called with us, he just walked in through the back door, and if we heard a quick step and a cheerful whistle in the hall, we knew that Sam had arrived. He was a frequent visitor and, being a bachelor, had to make his own meals, so he always enjoyed a bite with us. He used to say that no one could make tea like the lady of the manse – the title he always gave to Queenie!

In later life he became quite absent-minded and was sometimes so engrossed in his little problems that he was unaware of what was going on around him. On one occasion at a morning service, I announced the text on which I was going to preach, and Sam was supposed to have said, 'Oh no good, no good at all.' Those who heard this loud whisper assured me that he wasn't referring to my text but to some problem around his homestead, but I had my doubts! Certainly if he had the text in mind, the remark was entirely out of character for no minister ever had a more supportive and sympathetic elder.

On the morning following the death of Dick Shepherd, the well-known London pastor and broadcaster, two workmen on a bus noticed a poster announcing his death. One, in a sad voice, said, 'Poor Dick, we'll hear him no more.' 'Don't call him 'poor',' said his mate, 'won't God be glad to have him?' So with Sam Ferguson, if heaven is inhabited with souls like him, then not only will we have fellowship divine with the Lord but also glorious fellowship with the redeemed.

3

Divine Healing – Initiation

It is often said that first impressions are important. I am sure this is true but sometimes they can be very misleading. Certainly my first impressions of Divine Healing might very well have turned me against it for all time. This is how it happened. I had in my congregation a girl, Emma, who suffered from epilepsy. When she was a child her mother was able to cope very well but as she got older she became just too heavy to lift if she happened to fall in an attack, and as this had become a common occurrence, it was for the family a very worrying situation.

At that time I heard about a man who was described as a 'healer' and who was apparently having wonderful results. I thought he might be able to help and after a chat with the family we decided to seek his ministry. I contacted him and a date was arranged for his visit. He duly arrived and I was quite impressed by his confidence and assurance that the girl would be completely cured. We went up to her home and he told us something of his work and the amazing results of his ministry. Then he prayed with Emma, placing his hands on her head.

After this he assured the parents that Emma would never have another attack of epilepsy. Naturally all were delighted, especially Emma, who saw a new world opening up to her; owing to her illness she had been unable to live a normal social life like other teenagers, even going to Church had not been possible for some years.

If what I had witnessed and been told had been all bona fide then I too would have seen a new world ahead where God would be using people to perform miraculous cures as in the days of Jesus, but it was not to be. In the home, preparations were undertaken to equip Emma for her new life. Next day, Tuesday, she was taken to town to get a new outfit with a view to going to Church on Sunday. Alas, on Friday, the attacks returned and were as bad as ever. The family contacted me and I went to the home immediately. It wasn't a pleasant visit for although the parents were not annoyed with me for bringing the 'healer', they were terribly disappointed mainly on Emma's

*The interior of Sinclair Seamen's Church, Belfast, where Rev J.A. McFarland
pioneered the Church's Ministry of Healing. Note the many emblems of life at sea.*

account, the poor girl had just gone to pieces. I tried to bring a little comfort
and hope but I could see that damage had been done that would take a long
time to put right. The effect on me was predictable; I just decided that if this
was a sample of Divine Healing then I had had enough of it.

But there was a higher hand working behind the scene. Some time after
this I moved to Belfast and happened one day to visit a lady who was suffering
from a frozen shoulder. She told me in great detail how it affected her, she
couldn't do her hair, tie on her apron and at night had to take a number of
sleeping pills to get even a few hours' sleep.

Then having come to the end of her catalogue of trials, she suddenly stopped
and asked me a question which she seemed to feel had a bearing on what she
had told me. 'What about these healing services in Sinclair Seamen's Church?'
At that time the minister of this church. Rev James McFarland, had organised
a monthly healing service, probably the first to be held in our Presbyterian
Church. It was a courageous thing to do for many of our people felt that this
ministry might be all right in certain sects but there was no place for it in the

tradition and theology of our Church. But when people see things happen or perhaps face a crisis in life, opinions can alter and I'm glad to say that James McFarland lived to see a remarkable change of attitude to this ministry.

Perhaps my old friend realised that James was on the right track, hence the question. My reply was that I wasn't involved and didn't know much about these services. 'Well,' she said, 'You are a minister and you ought to be taking part in this work; now just come over here and put your hand on my shoulder and pray for me.' That certainly took me by surprise but the lady in question was a retired schoolteacher and the members of that profession are accustomed to giving orders and having them obeyed – at least that is how it used to be!

So I did what I was told, somewhat reluctantly, placing my hands on her shoulder and saying a simple prayer for healing. As I left for home I felt rather like a cheat for I had done something that I wasn't prepared for and I certainly knew that I wasn't equipped for such a specialised ministry.

However, next morning I had to visit the local school and during my absence the lady rang up and told my wife that her shoulder was completely cured, she was able to do her hair and tie her apron without pain and had slept all night without painkillers! She lived for some ten years after that and had no further pain in her shoulder.

In view of my previous disappointing experience, I felt that this was the hand of the Lord giving me a wee nudge toward the healing ministry. I accepted this guidance and eventually became responsible for organising the Sinclair Seamen's services.

I must acknowledge that down the years I have seldom seen such sudden and dramatic results as in the case of the frozen shoulder but enough has happened to make me absolutely sure that Christ through His Spirit is active in the fight against disease as in the days of His flesh, and if we don't often see wonderful healing miracles, maybe it is because we are in a Nazareth situation, where He could do no mighty work because of unbelief. This coupled with the fact that He has to use as channels of His healing love, people like myself who are very conscious of our weakness and unworthiness.

4

Three Men of the Cloth

I have always had an interest in people who were different from the rest of us. We sometimes refer to these as 'characters', people who have attitudes and ways of life that we don't regard as quite normal. Such may not be as common as in the past yet in most spheres, not least the Christian ministry, they are still to be found.

Three such come to mind all of whom have influenced me in various ways. In the following thumb-nail sketches of these special people I do not attempt to give a full picture of their character but simply make a brief reference to the trait that I saw as outstanding in their make-up.

Rev W.J. Craney

The first is the minister of my youth, Rev W.J. Craney of Loanends. He was a very gifted person with varied interests, music, literature, photography and gardening. As a pastor he was kind and thoughtful and in the pulpit his sermons and prayers were of a high standard. Occasionally as he led his people in prayer, he sounded like a man possessed by the spirit of the Lord. Moving and inspiring thoughts flowed from his lips. Afterwards he might casually remark to a friend, 'This was the day of the beautiful prayers,' but he couldn't recall any of them.

However, he was well known for something else – his sense of humour and gift of razor-sharp repartee. Many examples could be quoted but I mention only a few. One evening 'W.J.' as we knew him arrived at my home with a friend, Rev David McKinney of Dundrod, by no means a slow witted person. It was a great joy for me, a schoolboy, and for my family, to listen to the battle of wits as these two friends tried to score points against each other. In those days ministers usually referred to each other by surname. How different the position today when even in Presbytery meetings ministers are often referred to as Jimmy or Willie, etc. Probably this is in keeping with the informality of our modern age but I'm not sure that it adds to the standing of the clergy. So back to Craney and McKinney. At that time the minimum salary was around £250 per year and both ministers felt it was too small. 'Craney,' said McKinney, 'if you and I had gone into business we would have been earning a thousand a year.' 'Ah no,' was 'W.J.'s' reply. 'You might have been earning a thousand a year, but I would have been earning two thousand a year!'

On another occasion at a funeral, 'W.J.' was speaking to a woman who was rather annoyed because he had never called at her home – pastoral visitation was not the strongest element in his ministry! 'Mr Craney,' she said, 'I suppose you don't know me although I'm a member of your church.' 'W.J.' looked at her carefully for a moment and then said in his usual calm voice, 'No. I don't seem to know you. I certainly never saw you in my church.' End of conversation for she seldom, if ever, attended church!

The following I heard from my father who had been attending a meeting of church committee. He was always careful not to discuss committee business with the family but this little item was so good it had to be shared. On this occasion the committee had been discussing a rather serious problem and were agreed as to how it should be solved, with one exception who had different ideas. He argued his point very forcefully but at length realised his cause was lost and he didn't like it. He rose abruptly from his seat and made for the door. As he opened it to leave he turned round and had a parting shot at the members of committee. 'You're just a pack of fools,' he muttered, but before the door closed behind him, like an arrow came the response from the chairman 'W.J.', 'Well there's one less now!'

But undoubtedly one of the most outstanding examples of his wit occurred one night at a social function in a neighbouring church when the local school-teacher was being honoured after some forty years of faithful service and, of course, Craney's humour was all impromptu.

Many wonderful tributes were paid to the guest of honour and as sometimes happens on these occasions one or two of the speakers had been perhaps over-lavish in their appreciation so much so that the teacher was somewhat overcome and in his reply made an unfortunate remark. 'I understand,' he said, 'in the Church of Rome that when a person is being canonized there is always present the Devil's Advocate. His commission is to bring up anything that might be weak or sinful in the life of the one to be canonized.' And then he added, 'In view of all that has been said about me tonight, if I were ever in this position the Devil's Advocate would be redundant.'

That remark didn't go unnoticed by 'W.J.' After a sumptuous supper he was asked to express thanks to the ladies for their hospitality; this little job often came his way. However, when he rose to his feet his thoughts were not with the ladies: he had other things in mind. I have to point out that the teacher had been a dedicated member of his church and having taught most of the members of kirk session and committee he was a man of considerable authority in the church – to these office-bearers he was still 'the master'. The result was that he tended to run the show and did it quite well. This was on the whole accepted by the congregation, but with the minister it was rather different and sometimes tension and disagreement arose. 'W.J.' knew all about this and in a quiet voice began his speech. 'Our friend has stated that in his case the Devil's Advocate would have nothing to say. Well, I am the Devil's Advocate!' What followed brought the teacher gently down to earth as he was reminded in a very witty and clever manner of his failings down the years. Very few could have done this without causing offence but when 'W.J.' had finished all, including the teacher, were in fits of laughter. As a teenager from a neighbouring congregation I can't think why I was present but it was an occasion which I wouldn't have liked to miss.

'W.J.'s' sense of humour continued to the end of the road. In his will he had drawn up instructions regarding his funeral. Only six people whom he named were to attend and after the funeral all six were to go to a certain hotel for the best lunch available, the cost to be included in funeral expenses. Then he stated that he had attended funerals for over forty years and had usually come home, cold and hungry. He did not want that to happen at his funeral!

Rev Joseph McKee

One lovely Sunday afternoon in August 1926, two cars arrived at the manse at Balteagh near Limavady. They contained a group of elders from the united charge of Redrock and Druminnis in County Armagh who were not out for a Sunday afternoon drive but were on a very definite mission – to obtain a minister for their vacant charge. We are told that Saint Patrick, while in France, had a vision and heard 'the voice of the Irish'. The minister of Balteagh, Rev

Joseph McKee was to have a rather similar experience not a vision but a visitation and in both cases the same plea, 'Come and walk amongst us once more.' Joseph had begun his ministry in Redrock.

In my word of introduction to this chapter I pointed out that I would be referring only to what I considered the outstanding trait in each personality. In the case of Joseph McKee it has to be his utter selflessness which came out very clearly in this situation. Let's think of some of the conditions in which he was pressed to make a very important decision about his future. There were three children in the McKee family, Agnes. Jean and Tom., and all had received a college education, Tom qualifying as a doctor. All this, of course, was done without any state assistance which meant a considerable drain on the family resources. But that was past and the parents could now begin to make some provision for retirement. There had been a very happy and successful ministry in Balteagh in which a fine church hall had been built and a very strong bond of affection formed between minister and people. The thought of removing to another charge was far from the mind of the minister and then out of the blue came this urgent appeal from a former congregation.

On the material side the Armagh deputation hadn't a lot to offer. The salary would be lower and the work probably more difficult. A union had recently been formed between Redrock and Druminnis and there were problems, mainly because for several years the congregation of Druminnis had been sadly neglected by their minister and many families had drifted away. On the other hand they represented a people who were completely agreed on one thing, that while there was a big job to be done, Rev Joseph McKee was the man who could do it. To say that they wouldn't take 'No' for an answer would be putting it too strongly but it came close to that!

Joseph thought and prayed much about it and after a few days decided to accept the invitation simply because he felt it must be the Lord's will that he should do so. And so in October 1926 there began a new ministry in Redrock and Druminnis which was blessed in many ways. For example the number of families in Druminnis more than doubled and Redrock was greatly strengthened during those sixteen years of dedicated service. It was towards the end of his ministry that I came to know him and later had the privilege of being called to succeed him in this united charge, aware of the well-nigh impossible task of maintaining the lofty standards set by my predecessor.

His spirit of selflessness continued into retirement. At that time the senior

One of the Churches to which Rev Joseph McKee returned, Redrock.

minister was entitled to live on in the manse for the remainder of his days. He had no intention of doing that for he felt it would be unfair to his successor and so his first job was to buy a small house in Belfast, thus making the manse available for me. When that happened the retired minister was entitled to £50 in lieu of manse. In this case it was agreed by the union commission that Redrock would pay £30 and Druminnis £20 annually to the senior minister. At the end of the first year the amounts were duly forwarded to him, but in each case he returned £10, feeling that he would become a burden on the congregations. It must be pointed out that in all this selflessness Mrs McKee was fully behind him showing the same spirit and prepared to make the same sacrifices.

Joseph had suffered for many years with a stomach ulcer which had become steadily worse making surgery necessary. At that time such surgery was postponed as long as possible. I went to see him in hospital on the Thursday

The other Church to which Rev McKee returned, Druminnis, later succeeded by the author.

of Holy Week 1943. He was in a very weak condition but his faith was strong. 'They're going to operate on Sunday morning,' he said, 'that's Easter Sunday morning. Our Lord received new life on the first Easter morn and I believe that this may happen to me.' Well, it did. The ulcer that all were concerned about proved to be benign and he lived for almost twenty years after that. During these years he seemed to find it difficult to accept the whole concept of retirement – that he should be maintained by church and state without having to render any service in return! And as a result he was forever trying to make some contribution to the world around him. For example, instead of sending Christmas cards to his many friends, he sometimes sent a delightful Christmas meditation.

I remember one under the title, 'Emmanuel, God with us.' As you read it you realised that the writer was not one who observed Christmas just on 25th December, but for him Christmas, Emmanuel, God with us, was a glorious reality every day. This meant taking seriously the teaching of Jesus, especially that demanding saying: 'If any man will come after me, let him deny himself and take up his cross daily and follow me.'

I had the great privilege of giving the address at his funeral service in Redrock Church. I based my remarks on words from the Epistle to the Hebrews, 'He being dead yet speaketh.' My contribution on that occasion may have been very inadequate and is long forgotten, but these words still apply to Joseph McKee.

'He being dead yet speaketh.'

Dr Arnold Frank

While I made a brief reference to Dr Frank in my earlier book, I feel that so much more could be said about him and so much blessing has come to countless people from his ministry and Christ-like character, that I must include him in my little trilogy of clerical friends. I feel very honoured to have experienced his friendship.

I first met him in Assembly's College in the year 1940 when he came to address members of the Missionary Society. We had an excellent list of speakers that session, mainly missionaries, retired or on furlough, each with his own particular message and challenge, but one seemed to stand out from the rest, our 80 year old missionary to the Jewish people of Hamburg.

If we look for the outstanding trait in his character, it isn't hard to find – a burning desire, as a convert from Judaism, to share with others the peace, the joy, the salvation which he had found in Jesus Christ.

Arnold Frank was born on 6th March 1859, near the town of Rajecz in Hungary, one of a family of nine, the only Jewish family in a Roman Catholic village. At the age of 16 he was sent by his father to work in a bank in Hamburg where there was a strong Jewish community. Some years before this our Presbyterian Church had established missionary work amongst the Jews of this great city. Through what appeared to be a chance meeting, though the hand of God was in it all, he was invited to attend a service in the Jerusalem Church, our mission centre. From that moment he became interested in the Christian faith and after a term of concentrated study and much prayer, he dedicated his life to the Saviour. Those in charge of the mission realised that here was someone sent from God who seemed eminently qualified to be a leader in the future work of the mission. With his Jewish background, he could talk to Jews on a level which they would understand but most important, he could speak of a Saviour whom he knew on a personal basis.

After some years of study at Assembly's College he was ordained to the Christian ministry, planning to work at our Jewish Mission centre in Hamburg with his wife (Ella Louise Kinghan, daughter of the Rev John Kinghan, founder of the Kinghan Mission). The story of the ministry that followed is something that our church can take great pride in for Arnold Frank, assisted by his dedicated wife, gave himself without counting the cost and laboured seeking no reward save that of knowing that sheaves were being gathered in for the Lord's great harvest.

On the material side there was the building of the new Jerusalem Church, the nurses' home, the hospital and many other projects. While on the spiritual side there is no way of assessing the countless people, mainly Jews, whose lives had been touched and sometimes transformed by the ministry of this gracious man of God.

Then came the heart-breaking end to his work through the rise of Nazism and anti-Semitism. Because of the mission's close connection with the Jewish people it was under suspicion. The charge was that what the Mission stood for was contrary to Nazi ideology. As a result in September 1939, Dr Frank was interned and all the property was 'provisionally sequestrated'. The British Foreign Office took steps to have him freed but shortly after his release he was warned anonymously that he would be interned again and that he must leave the country. He realised that there was no other option, so sadly he and his family had to say goodbye to their many friends and the achievement of many years of hard work and set out for Belfast.

It was shortly after this time that he spoke to the students of Assembly's College and made such a deep impression on us all. Knowing something of his treatment by the Nazis we expected that he would naturally be embittered and hostile towards his persecutors, but this was not so. Instead we heard words that reminded us of Stephen who, as the stones rained down upon his head prayed, 'Lord, lay not this sin to their charge.' He just seemed to live on a higher level than the normal. I recall many years later telling him about being conned by a man who had called at our manse looking for help. I

Jerusalem Church and Nurses' Home built during Dr Frank's Ministry.

Jerusalem Church interior, damaged in air-raids in 1942.

expected sympathy, but not so, for with a gracious smile he simply said, 'It is better to be deceived than to misjudge a person.'

My last contact with him concerned a tape recorder. They had just become available at a reasonable price and I, with my weakness for new things, felt that I must buy one, on the pretext, of course, that it would be useful for Church work! At this time Dr Frank, now over 100 years of age, was finding it difficult to write letters and yet was so keen to keep in touch with his many friends, especially the workers in Hamburg.

We thought about the tape recorder and I took it to his home on several occasions. He recorded a message and the tape was posted to the leaders in the Jerusalem Church and hospital. When the reply came back I had the pleasure of hearing him translate messages from the various groups and coming through loud and clear was the strength of the bonds of love and esteem that made him their father in Christ.

Recently I had the privilege of spending some time reading a valuable possession of Arnold Frank, his pocket New Testament including the Book of Psalms. This he had with him during his days of internment and it brought him much strength and comfort during that brief but very trying time. The New Testament reveals God's love for man but this copy of Arnold Frank's revealed something else – the love of a man for his God. Many verses are underlined, especially those that proclaim the goodness and divinity of Jesus and His great love for the individual, something which the Saviour had obviously passed on to His servant, Arnold, for the driving power of his life was to win people for the Lord.

And as I thought of all this I was reminded of those lines, familiar to many of us, written about the great Scottish preacher, Samuel Rutherford, which portray the tremendous love he had for the people of his parish, Anwoth.

> 'Oh! if one soul from Anwoth meet me at God's right hand,
> Then heaven will be two heavens, in Emmanuel's land.'

And I believe that Arnold Frank would have had similar feelings towards the people to whom he ministered.

5

A Mother's Love

In spite of the tragic breakdown of family life which seems so prevalent in our modern society, in spite of the tensions that corrode the bonds of affection and the pressures that can destroy the happiness of a home, in spite of all these there is one quality which I believe will always survive – the love of a mother for her child. The following experience would support such a thought.

I was invited recently to conduct a Harvest Thanksgiving Service in a former congregation. After the service I spoke to the folk as they left, many of whom I hadn't seen for a very long time. Amongst them was a tall well-built man in his forties. He told me his name and it immediately rang a bell. It recalled a remarkable thing that had happened about forty years earlier and this is a brief account of that eventful night.

Just after midnight I received an urgent telephone call requesting me to go to the local hospital to baptise a baby boy who was dying. Some people are critical of parents who would be very concerned if their little one should die without being baptised. Personally I can understand that concern perhaps because I have seen the peace and comfort that often follow the sacramental act. The baby was seriously ill and his mother was struggling with the thought of his imminent death. I had a little chat with her and then went ahead with the baptism.

It was after this that difficulties arose. The mother took me aside and told me that it was her wish that, if the baby were to die that he should die at home. I tried to reason with her, pointing out the advantage of keeping the child in hospital but all to no avail. So reluctantly I went to the ward sister and explained the situation. She was naturally very disturbed about the idea of the child being taken from hospital. I remember her terse summing up, 'If the child is kept in hospital he has a faint chance of survival but if he is taken home there is no chance at all.'

Well, I thought that would settle the matter for mother, but not at all. I put the case to her as strongly and I hope, as lovingly as I could, but she was determined to take the child home right away and here I got more deeply involved. She asked me if I had my car and if I would take her and the baby home. We sometimes speak of being on the horns of a dilemma and that was my position at that moment. If I were to take the baby home and he died, the hospital staff would rightly take a dim view of my aiding and abetting, while on the other hand if he died in hospital the mother would feel that she had been let down by her minister. I thought hard for a few minutes and I probably said a little prayer for guidance. I have always found that helpful in moments of crisis. In the end I felt that the mother should have the major say in the matter and agreed to take her home with the baby in her arms. I have forgotten what the sister said when I told her what had been agreed but she wasn't too pleased and that's putting it mildly!

It was about 2.00 am when we got to the house, an old farmhouse with a big kitchen. The father was sitting at a log fire waiting anxiously for news. He was very confused when he saw the baby in his mother's arms and for an awful moment, thought the child was dead. He had been told earlier that he might not see the morning. However, the mother explained to him all that had happened and then putting the baby in the father's arms, went off to make a cup of tea, mainly with the minister in mind! I never fail to be amazed at the thoughtfulness of some people in times of crisis. The Bible provides us with a wonderful example of this – the day when Jesus ministered to Peter's mother-in-law who was ill with fever. After Jesus had healed her she rose immediately and began to prepare a meal for her visitors – no thought of all that she had come through but with a real concern for the needs of others.

So after we had had our cup of tea by the fireside, the mother sat down in the armchair, the only one that was at all comfortable. Then the baby was placed in her arms and seemed to enjoy the warmth of his mother's body as he snuggled in. Some of us have been brought almost to the end of our tether by the crying of a baby in the wee sma' hours! We would have loved to hear that baby cry as loud and as long as he felt like it, but not a sound came from those pale little lips. The mother sat there all night enveloping her child in a great blanket of warmth and love and prayer.

I called back in the morning and was delighted to find the child still alive and in fact noticeably stronger and brighter. He progressed steadily and grew up to be the strong healthy man to whom I had spoken after the Harvest Service. Most people would find it difficult to explain in medical and scientific terms how this remarkable recovery happened. I think we just have to move to a different dimension. Had the child been left in hospital he would have received the very best treatment and attention that was available. Nothing that might have saved his life would have been left undone, but it might not have been enough.

There is, it seems, a mystical bond between mother and child. It's there all the time but manifests itself in time of crisis and that may explain what happened during those agonizing hours. The bond became a channel of healing love that issued from the mother's heart and from the Saviour who told us that it was not the Father's will that one of these little ones should perish.

When St. Paul said, 'Now abideth, faith, hope and love, these three, but the greatest is love', I wonder if he could have envisaged a scene like this – the mother certainly had faith and she had a glimmer of hope but it was her great love that didn't fail. How much we owe to a mother's love, as the poet has put it in strong but touching words:

> *'If I were dammed in body and soul*
> *I know whose love would make me whole*
> *Mother o' mine.'*

6

Light in the Darkness

The year 1942 was a very depressing one for our nation. We were in the midst of the Second World War and things were going badly for the British. The Japs seemed unstoppable in the Far East; in February they captured Singapore and over 100,000 British and Commonwealth soldiers and airmen were made prisoner. Churchill described it as 'the worst disaster and largest capitulation in British military history'.

Rommel was giving our forces a tough time in the desert war and our vessels, crossing the Atlantic with food and vital supplies, were suffering heavy losses and appeared to be at the mercy of the German U-boats. At home rationing was becoming more severe and not only food and petrol but most things that we would normally regard as essential were becoming really scarce.

But the people never really lost hope or their sense of humour and lots of jokes went the rounds helping us to smile even in the darkest days. I recall, for example, at a time when food reserves were becoming dangerously low, Government put forward a DIY suggestion entitled 'Dig for Victory', implying that we should all try to produce some of our own food. Well, the story was told of a chap digging, not very enthusiastically, in his garden on a Saturday morning when a neighbour popped his head over the fence and quipped, 'Hello, Bill, are you diggin' for victory?' 'No,' replied Bill, pointing towards the kitchen where his wife was at work, 'I'm diggin' for peace!'

I recall another 'crack' which caused many a smile at that time. Of course, there was no T.V. to entertain us, just the 'wireless', and one programme that certainly did not cheer us up was a news commentary from Germany by an offensive character who became known as Lord Haw Haw. We didn't have to listen to him but many were tempted to turn him on at times and he became the man whom we loved to hate! He would tell us of all the ships that had been lost in the Atlantic, of the countless British planes that had been shot down, that we were facing imminent starvation and that we should surrender right away! Now the story went round that one Saturday evening a farmer's wife was preparing for tea with a well filled pan on the cooker, eggs, bacon, potato bread etc., while Lord Haw Haw in the background kept talking about the starving British. She put up with it for a while but then, losing her temper, she grabbed the pan and holding it close to the 'wireless' shouted, 'Well, if we're starving, just you smell that!'

But there were other sources of light and hope and one of these was a visit of King George VI and Queen Elizabeth on June 25th to Armagh. This was part of a tour of American troops based in the province and for security reasons had to be kept very hush-hush. For example, in the Belfast News Letter, report of the visit to the Armagh base isn't even mentioned. But locally the word got around that a very important person would be visiting our city on a certain day and hurried arrangements got under way. Some time before this I had joined the recently formed branch of the St John's Ambulance Association – everyone felt that we must do something to help, especially as air-raids were still a real possibility. All the members of our company had passed various tests and had received certificates informing us that we were now qualified to render first aid to the injured. We were delighted when we learnt that we would be on stand-by duty at this important event and turned up, very proud in our new uniforms! But alas, in spite of the heat and excitement, no one fainted or was injured so our services weren't called upon! The only casualty was a member of our company who got a severe headache and had to withdraw!

The event lasted less than an hour but in that time the Royal couple came to realise something of the love and esteem in which they were held by the people of Armagh and district. It was also a tremendous boost to the morale of us all. But when the fuss and excitement were over we experienced a feeling of anti-climax, not unusual on such occasions – we were 'all dressed up and no place to go!' However, my friend Wm McCappin, later to become Bishop of Connor, had the answer; he had met some friends from Dublin who had rushed up at the last minute to see the Royal visitors and who were not in a hurry to leave.

So he suggested that we have 'a bite to eat' – that's how one described a cafe meal in wartime – no one ever had to complain of plates being too full. Afterwards we decided to take our friends to Navan Fort. There wasn't much to see there, just a grassy mound surrounded by a ditch, but William had done some research and regaled us with tales about the ancient kings of Ireland

Luncheon Party at Stormont before tour of the American Army Bases. The King and Queen were guests of the Prime Minister and Mrs Andrews. Also in the group are the Governor and Duchess of Abercorn, the Marquess of Londonderry and Mr R. Gransden, Secretary to the Ulster Cabinet.

The First Aid Team proud of their new uniform and St John Ambulance Brigade badge!

who had been crowned here. So in one afternoon we had been in contact with the present monarchy and that of some 2000 years previous!

The next bright spot in that summer was the annual lawn-tennis tournament organised by the County Club. It was a most enjoyable occasion; no one took the tennis tournament too seriously, but it was followed by a delightful supper – much appreciated in those days of rationing. There was also the opportunity for those who were bachelors of meeting some very attractive young ladies! The two photos of the same club with exactly half-a-century separating them, show how tennis attire and general fashions have evolved. We smile at the older one, the big hats, boaters and bow-ties seem to indicate a greater interest in appearance than in the ability to play tennis! We may also be amused at the later one; today, another half-century later the white flannels and tennis

A group taking part in a Lawn-Tennis Tournament at the County Club in 1892, and, below, players and friends who took part in a similar Tournament at the County Club 50 years later.

frocks have been replaced by shorts and the briefest of skirts. No one knows what the next half-century will produce in this sphere but there's not much room left for adjustments!

While the folk in the older photo are a little before my time, I can name nearly all in the more recent one. In the front row are a number of prominent local people, including Lady Stronge, Miss McClintock of Fellowes Hall, Canon Bloomer of St Mark's and Rev A. W. Neill of First Armagh. Those in the back row are perhaps less important but include a well-known police sergeant who was renowned for his expertise in catching criminals and for his intense fear of mice! Throughout the long demanding struggle it was important to maintain the morale of the people at home and activities such as this played an important part.

But light was available at a deeper level and in the autumn a number of church leaders came together and decided to hold a mission, with the purpose of giving people greater spiritual strength to face the possible suffering and uncertainty of the future. The well known evangelist. Tom Rees, was chosen to be chief speaker and he gladly agreed. He was an excellent choice, his sincerity and enthusiasm making a deep impression on the people. I had the privilege of taking him round some of our schools and institutions and the abiding memory I have of these visits is that when he met people who were complete strangers to him, he treated them as old friends!

I have forgotten his sermons but I remember one of his texts, it was Revelation Ch. 19 v 6 'Alleluia, for the Lord God omnipotent reigneth'. It brought a message that the people needed very much and many were confirmed in their faith and better able to face the days ahead. They had certainly been drawn closer to the Christ who said, 'I am the light of the world.'

Fifty years later, in a world where we have made fantastic progress, materially and scientifically, but seem to have lost our way spiritually, this message is even more relevant; we need its comfort, its challenge and its glorious hope for all mankind.

'Alleluia, for the Lord God omnipotent reigneth.'

7

Gary

Recently while looking through an old scrap-book I came across a press cutting which carried a brief article on a very remarkable child called Gary. He had been adopted (or should I say chosen?) when he was just two years of age and in very poor health. His new mother, a nurse, did a wonderful job and gradually Gary became a strong, healthy child, full of fun and mischief, apparently a 'Just William' type.

When he was about ten years of age, however, he began to lose something of his zest for living and complained about being tired. After various tests in hospital it was confirmed that he was suffering from leukaemia. Following the usual treatment there was no improvement in his condition and the parents, desperately keen that he should live, decided to take him to a top consultant in London. Here they received really sad news – the leukaemia was a very severe type and it was feared that Gary would live, at most, only a few months.

The parents were devastated. A friend suggested that they should contact someone in the Church's ministry of healing and my name was mentioned. I agreed to visit the child and hoped to be able to help the parents also in their heart-breaking situation. Gary won my heart from the first moment that I saw him, his happy smile and dancing eyes, in spite of constant pain, convinced me that this was a very special child. I knew nothing of the background of the family as regards spiritual matters and so began my chat with Gary carefully feeling my way. 'Gary,' I said, 'Have you heard about Jesus?' Like a shot came back the reply, 'Of course I have, sure He is with me all the time.' After that it was easy and a great privilege to minister to Gary. I told him that Jesus sometimes used my hands to make people well and to remove pain. I then explained to him that I would place my hands on his tummy where the pain was most severe, that we would be quiet for a little while and then we would all pray that Jesus would take away that awful pain.

Gary seemed to understand perfectly and with the faith of a child – would that we grown-ups could have such faith – he accepted every word I said, obviously hoping for something special from Jesus. After a little while he opened his eyes and whispered, 'It's going away.' The pain was certainly decreasing and inside an hour was completely gone. For two days he required no pain-killers, but then the severe pain returned and he had to be taken to the Children's Hospital. By this time the leukaemia had spread and drugs seemed to be less effective. Gary had been a wonderful patient but he could really take no more. 'Mummy,' he said, 'Get the man with the nice hands.'

His father rang me right away but unfortunately we were about to visit some friends. In a case like this real friends understand if plans are upset and so it was here. In a very short time I was on my way to see Gary.

In spite of his pain he managed a faint smile and I realized that he was critically ill. Again my hands were placed on his tummy and for a time there was no change, he just seemed to appreciate the feeling of warmth. Then something wonderful happened. He looked up and gave us a lovely smile as he said, 'It's gone.' The pain returned next morning but much less severe and not requiring pain killers. Two days later Gary passed peacefully away. All who knew him felt a deep sense of loss. I called at the home after the funeral and was very impressed by the faith and courage that the parents were showing as they faced life without their darling son.

There is a rather interesting sequel to this moving story. Some weeks later I was suffering from a severe head-cold and Queenie, like all good wives, ever watchful of her husband's well-being, insisted that I spend the morning in bed! Reluctantly I agreed and after a time fell into a sound sleep. On waking up, for some reason I turned on the radio. As I listened I got quite a surprise for two ladies were discussing Divine Healing and I was even more surprised to learn that they were actually talking about me! I soon realized that Gary's mother was being interviewed by someone from the B.B.C. and they were discussing the effect of the great sorrow that had descended upon the home as a result of Gary's death. His mother recalled how the thought of parting with Gary was really breaking their hearts. They had tried everything and then in desperation they resorted to the prayer healing ministry.

As I listened I thought of the ministry of Jesus and of at least two cases where people turned to Him in sheer desperation, the woman who touched the hem of His garment and the blind man in Jericho. In both cases Jesus seemed to understand their feelings of despair and certainly rewarded them handsomely. I tend to think that the casual prayer seldom gets through the ceiling but the Lord's ear is ever attentive to the prayer of desperation.

Gary's mother then gave a brief account of my visits and their outcome. The interviewer didn't seem to be greatly impressed by this as she put the question, 'You brought this man along, he prayed with Gary but he died, surely this must have broken down your faith in prayer, even in God?' 'No,' was the reply, 'just the reverse. My husband and I now have a stronger faith and we are certainly closer to God than we were before.'

Most people would regard the aim of Divine Healing as the bringing of health to someone who is ill. It is much more than that, it is the bringing of Christ into every situation where there is dis-ease, and when that happens we get a little glimpse of Heaven, as broken hearts are bound up and tears are wiped away.

'Thine be the glory, risen, conquering Son.'

8

Fringe Medicine

To say that men are more intelligent than women is somewhat controversial, but there is a sphere in which the 'more' can be used without a murmur of opposition from the ladies, and that is when coupled with the words 'obstinate' or 'pig-headed'. This is especially so in times of sickness – a husband may be quite ill and when his good wife suggests a day in bed the obstinate creature won't hear of it, and as regards sending for the doctor, that is quite out of the question!

Well, early in my ministry I got a bad bout of 'flu which I was sure I would be able to fight off without going to bed, but it didn't work that way. On Saturday morning my home-help, Sadie, advised me strongly to see my doctor, but I assured her that I would be all right and fit for work next day which included conducting a morning service in Cookstown, some thirty miles distant. As the day went on I certainly didn't improve and had a nose bleed which went on for quite a long time. Some hours later it returned and this time it may not have poured but it was certainly a persistent trickle. I tried all the usual remedies but the bleeding continued. As a last resort I lay flat on the floor which meant that a lot of blood trickled down my throat with unpleasant consequences.

Eventually it stopped but I felt very weak and knew that I wouldn't be fit for my work next morning. I happened to know that Rev James Woods, assistant in the Mall Church, Armagh, was free on that Sunday and might be prepared to go to Cookstown, but alone in the Manse and without a telephone, how was I to get in touch with him? Possibly I prayed for help for I was in a desperate situation. Some time later, to my great relief, a neighbour called to enquire about me – news travels fast in the country! He kindly agreed to contact James Woods who never hesitated about helping me out, very much 'a friend in need'.

There was, however, a rather amusing outcome from this arrangement. James Woods was a master of the English language and always spoke with great precision but tended never to use a small word where a big one would be applicable! Before leaving for Cookstown he called at the Mall Church and happened to speak to the church officer. He told him about the arrangement – that he was going to take a service in Cookstown in my place as I was ill. He referred to my illness as a severe haemorrhage. The church officer wasn't sure but he fancied that it must have been in the brain, and then it all began to snowball. Soon it was being said that I would never be able to preach again and that if I did pull through, I would he an invalid for life!

The result was that on the Sunday afternoon, people tip-toed up to the manse door, almost afraid to ring the bell. They got quite a shock when the door was opened by the minister, looking perhaps a little pale but in fairly normal health!

But worse was to follow. The large amount of blood which I had swallowed had upset things inside and by Monday my desire for food had gone completely and a strange yellowness had appeared in my eyes. I didn't need a doctor to tell me that I had got jaundice! I felt very depressed but hoped that it would soon clear up. However, by Wednesday morning there was no improvement and Sadie, always keen to help, told me that a neighbour, Mrs Dickson, had a cure for jaundice, but she thought that I wouldn't take it. 'Well.' I said, 'It's like this, if I don't get a cure soon, I'll probably die!' That was certainly how I felt, so I decided to try this 'cure' and Mrs Dickson set off through the fields collecting various herbs for the mixture. It had an awful taste but having heard great reports about its efficacy, I managed to get it down. Almost immediately after the first dose I began to feel better and two days later my doctor, a personal friend, called to see me. I think he had heard of 'the severe haemorrhage!' He was a little suspicious of my eyes but passed me as fit and I was able to conduct my services on the following Sunday. I didn't dare tell him about my cure' although he was the kind of person who would have understood and would have seen the funny side of it all.

This little episode has a bearing upon the Divine Healing ministry. An important aspect of the theology of this ministry is that God is behind every healing agent. Jesus seemed to regard disease as alien to the Father's Will. He never said to anyone who was sick, 'I'm sorry, I can't heal you because it is my Father's Will that you should be like this.' Instead He used every means available to combat sickness. Sometimes it was a word of command, sometimes the touch of His hand and on one occasion He even made a mixture

of saliva and dust with which He anointed the eyes of a blind man. From this
we can surely conclude that today He is still supportive of those who strive
to lift the burden of pain and to bring healing to bodies and minds diseased.
This applies to the brain surgeon performing a most delicate operation, to the
doctor coping with the everyday ills of his patients, to the nurse as she strives
to restore health and ease pain, to the minister bringing a spiritual dimension
into every diseased situation, to the many prayer groups who are channels of
the Saviour's healing love and to the old country woman as she gathered
herbs in the fields around her home to help a sick neighbour.

All are part of the team of Him who said, 'I am the Lord that healeth thee.'

9

Scary Moments

Most of us at some time have had the experience of being almost petrified by something that was very frightening or even threatening; and if we ourselves haven't been face to face with a ghost or spent a night in a haunted house with all kinds of bizarre things happening, we have probably talked to people who claim to have had such experiences. I have had my share of these but all were capable of explanation and yet they could easily have been regarded as belonging to the psychic world. As a result I feel that most of those hair-raising experiences, when thoroughly investigated, can be satisfactorily explained. In support of this view I mention a few personal incidents.

The first occurred shortly after my ordination. I was living alone in the large manse at Redrock, a considerable distance from my nearest neighbour. The local rector and I had decided to form a boys' club in the area, and on this particular night he had given me a lift to a meeting where we were to discuss the matter.

He stopped at my gate-way and after further conversation about our venture, I left his car and feeling rather cold began to walk briskly up the avenue towards the manse. As I headed for the back door I could see a figure in white coming towards me. By this time it was almost midnight and quite dark. My pace certainly slowed as the figure approached and I was about to start walking backwards when a voice said, 'Is that you. Mr McComb?' It wasn't the voice of a ghost but of a neighbour who lived up the road!

And this was the explanation of his strange appearance. His father had died suddenly and he was keen, for various reasons, to contact me as soon as possible. He had come down earlier and finding no one at home, decided to try later. I should point out that he was a man who never went out without his cap, summer or winter. On his second visit to the manse, his cap could not be found – there had been a lot of people coming and going and it had been mislaid. However, determined not to go without a head covering, he simply picked up a long white scarf and tied it under his chin, covering his head and shoulders and falling almost to his knees! It never seemed to occur to him that his appearance might be a little unusual! Certainly if I hadn't received this explanation and instead, had run for my life – although I was so scared that I doubt if my legs would have carried me far – I would afterwards have been hard to convince that I hadn't seen a ghost in my back yard!

My second incident of this nature took place in very different circumstances. By this time I was happily married and our first child, a baby daughter had just arrived. This was the first birth at Redrock manse for many years and caused quite a lot of interest in the congregation. There were two old sisters who were especially excited about it and my wife felt it would be a good idea to invite them to the manse some afternoon for a chat and a look at the wee one. So a date was fixed and I duly arrived at their home to do the necessary taxi-work. I should point out that these dear ladies, like most of us, had certain little peculiarities. For one thing they felt that their neighbours weren't at all friendly and showed this in various ways such as leaving gates open, breaking down fences, and borrowing tools and forgetting to return them. They might have described the last complaint in different wording! This, of course, was all largely in their imagination as I knew the neighbours very well and they were all decent, honest people.

When I arrived that afternoon there was quite a lot of activity around the home. Doors and windows were being checked and various things were being picked up and locked away. Eventually it was felt that all was safe and they then began to dress. This for them was an important occasion and after a considerable time they appeared attired in their best hats, with scarves, gloves etc. all in very good taste.

They were delighted to see little Heather who happened to be on her best behaviour. It was really a very interesting time for us all as they had spent many years in U.S.A. and had much to talk about. But from time to time there would be an expression of fear concerning what might be going on around their homestead while they were away.

The afternoon passed quickly and they felt that they should return before it became too dark; after many expressions of thanks for our little act of kindness, I got them safely back to their home and it was then that the trouble started. The key for the back door couldn't be found and the front door had been barred from the inside. The sisters had quite a heated argument as to where it had been left, one saying that it had been put in the coal house while the other insisted that it had been left on a shelf in the feeding house. In the end both agreed that it must have been stolen!

Meantime I had noticed that the porch had a flat roof and the adjoining window was partly open, and it struck me that with the help of a ladder I might be able to get to it and through it into the house. A ladder was available and after some manipulation I was able to get the window sufficiently open to let me through but it had to be head first! This meant that I fell in a heap on the floor of the landing. After picking myself up I stood for a moment to get my bearings and to my horror just across the landing, I saw the figure of a man. By this time it was almost dark and in view of all that I had heard earlier I jumped to the conclusion that it was an intruder! Putting on a show of composure I said in a loud voice, 'What are you doing here?' There was no answer and no movement, and as my eyes became accustomed to the darkness, I made an embarrassing discovery – on the opposite wall was a large mirror and the figure which I saw in it was my own! Feeling very shocked but relieved I came downstairs and let the two distraught sisters into their home, through the front door which had bars, strong enough for a fortress. I was careful, of course, not to refer to the scare upstairs!

I thought afterwards, if on seeing the 'figure', on the landing, I had bolted back through the window, as I was tempted to do, and raised the alarm that there was a man in the house. The result would have been drastic. Possibly there would have been a police search and when no trace of an intruder could be found, the obvious conclusion would have been that either the minister was seeing things or the house was haunted. From my own point of view if I hadn't discovered the explanation of the 'figure' on the landing, I would have had difficulty in believing that it was just a figment of my imagination. Again the importance of investigating all 'appearances!'

Another frightening moment was again quite different. This happened in the summer of 1952. In those days few ministers were able to go far afield for holidays owing to travel restrictions and in most cases, limited income, and some, especially those with a family, were very pleased to be offered a manse near the sea for a month. This, of course, meant that the minister was responsible for all Sunday services, while his wife found no escape from the sink, shopping and cooking!

However, a manse, in this case Dunluce, was available in lieu of our services and we really enjoyed the change. But it was remarkable how quickly the word got around that we were in residence in Dunluce manse, resulting in quite an influx of friends and relatives! This was very pleasant but added considerably to the chores of the lady of the house. The time passed quickly and as we had a wedding in our home congregation on the 28th of the month, we decided not to return to Dunluce for the final two days.

On our arrival home we found everything in order, the weeds had grown apace and there was plenty of work to be done in garden and grounds. Eventually we got to bed and about 3.00 am I woke up hearing voices and footsteps at the rear of the house. Getting up, I pulled the curtains and looked out, just in time to see two figures disappear into what we called the store. In the old days when ministers did a little farming, it had been used to store oats, potatoes, feeding stuff etc., and the name had lived on. In many little incidents in my life, the old saying could be applied, 'Fools rush in where angels fear to tread', and it was certainly relevant here. Without a gun, stick or even a torch, I slipped on my dressing-gown and went down to investigate, while my wife watched nervously from our bedroom window.

As I moved towards the store I heard movements inside and suddenly the door opened and out bolted two burly policemen, who were sure they had caught a burglar! This is how the confusion occurred. Before going on holiday, I had told the local police that we would be away for the month and would be grateful if they could keep an eye on the manse. As it happened, unknown to them, we had come home two days early and these officers of the law, doing their job carefully, had walked round the house, and then decided to rest a while in the store! They came in for a cup of tea and a chat and we all had a laugh as we saw the funny side of the situation.

However, if I hadn't investigated, I might today be telling my grandchildren about that night when I saw two dark figures disappear into an out-house at our home – what an opening for a ghost story!

10

Things that may hinder Healing

If we discuss the question of healing at any depth we soon find ourselves confronted by the ancient and modern problem – the cause of disease. Medical science devotes vast sums of money, employing the ablest people available, in a great campaign to solve this problem and progress is certainly being made and one day, hopefully, diseases like cancer and M.S. will be as curable as T.B.

Meantime we note that the Old Testament writers put forward a simple solution, making it clear that disease was due to sin. The classic example of this would be the occasion in the wilderness when the Israelites because of the hardships they were suffering – they were short of food and water – turned their backs completely upon God. They paid dearly for their sin, for the Lord sent serpents among them and there was great suffering, many dying; here and elsewhere it seemed to be accepted that sin and suffering go hand in hand. We find an echo of this in the Book of Job, his 'comforters' hinting that he must have been quite a lad in his younger days to have such suffering inflicted upon him. But Jesus takes a very different view as in dealing with the blind man. His disciples, brought up in the Old Testament tradition, took it for granted that the man's affliction must be due to sin. It was just a matter of apportioning the blame, hence the question, 'Who sinned, this man or his parents that he was born blind?' 'Neither,' replied Jesus, making it clear that in this case sin had no part to play. There was, of course, the man at the Pool of Bethesda to whom our Lord said, 'Go and sin no more lest a worse thing befall you,' but earlier in this account it is implied that Jesus knew the man's background and is simply warning him that if he returns to his evil ways, the paralysis could come back and be worse than ever.

In these two cases Jesus is making it very clear that while sin can certainly cause disease there are many cases of sickness where the cause will be found elsewhere. Today we realise more and more that good health depends upon the keeping of laws such as those concerning food, hygiene, physical exercise etc. I recall a rather stout lady coming to one of our services; she wanted to

41

lose three stones. I asked her if she had been to see her doctor. Of course I have,' she said, 'and he put me on a very strict diet, but I love sweet stuff!' She seemed to think that we would say a little prayer for her and she would lose three stones and continue eating sweet stuff! Well, Divine Healing doesn't work that way for Jesus said, 'Thou shalt not tempt the Lord thy God.' In other words, we break His laws at our peril, be they moral, mental or physical. This applies not only on a personal level but also on a communal one. The spate of hatred and violence that has pervaded our Province in recent years has brought untold suffering not least to innocent folk. So I would stress that people should not get the idea that suffering is the result of their sin; so often the reverse seems to be the case, really good people at times suffer greatly while the rascals appear to have perfect health.

At the same time I have to point out that there are things that might be called sinful attitudes which can delay healing. May I mention two cases that support this idea. The first began at an annual meeting in my congregation. Business had been completed and the ladies were about to serve supper when there was a power failure. All lights went out except the emergency ones in the main hall so we knew that if some form of light could be obtained for the kitchen the supper could be served. My car was near the kitchen door and I saw that the headlamps would provide sufficient light if the car were in the proper position. I was in the process of manoeuvring it round when someone tapped on the car window. A stranger was standing there and before I could speak to him he asked me if I had a cure for psoriasis! Ministers are never supposed to say naughty words but sometimes they are tempted! I certainly was on that occasion. However, I kept fairly calm, assuring him that I had no cure for psoriasis but if he wished to come at a more convenient season I would be glad to talk to him. We arranged a time for him to come to the manse next morning when we had a long chat about his skin trouble and his environment.

As we talked it became fairly clear that the cause of the trouble just might be his mother-in-law, not by any means a new problem! The position was that he had married and gone to live with his wife and her mother who owned the house. Now this might have worked all right if mother-in-law had been wise, but she wasn't. From time to time she made it clear that the house was hers and that she was in control. This annoyed him greatly as he was an independent type, but he was able to control his tongue and his feelings, albeit at the same time coping with civil war deep within himself. After weeks of severe tension in the home he noticed a skin rash on his arms which was later diagnosed as a form of psoriasis. Medication was specified but the complaint continued. He was really surprised when I told him that the trouble might have been caused by the poor relationship between him and his mother-in-law. Eventually he agreed that there might be a connection here but couldn't see how things could be changed. He wasn't a person who prayed so that avenue couldn't be used, but in the end he agreed to make a new start in the home accepting the fact that he was really just a lodger there. I never saw him again but he called at the manse about two months later. Unfortunately, I wasn't at home, but he was in great form and told my wife that the atmosphere in the home had changed completely and he and mother-in-law were getting on 'like a house on fire', then he added, 'and believe it or not, the psoriasis has almost completely disappeared'. Some may question the connection between the tension – due to wrong attitudes – and the disease, but our friend in the end had no doubts about it.

The second case occurred several years earlier in Belfast. After a healing service I spoke to a woman to whom we had ministered. She suffered from depression and had tried every available means of healing including attending several healing services but the burden of tension and depression wasn't lifted.

I was guided to ask her a rather searching question. 'Is there anything in your mind or in your life that you aren't happy about?' I knew that she was a keen Christian and a dedicated church worker. For a moment she didn't reply but blushed and was a little embarrassed. I assured her that if there was something, I didn't want to know about it but I felt that she should try to get this thing sorted out. Well, she insisted on telling me the whole story and it was really heart-breaking. A friend, so-called, had wronged her terribly and as a result her whole life had been affected and naturally it had left a legacy of bitterness. Most of us, I'm sure, in a similar situation would have reacted in the same way. Reconciliation seemed out of the question, the idea of going to her 'friend' with an olive branch offering forgiveness appeared unthinkable. All I could think of was to ask her to pray for grace to do this. She agreed to pray but she wasn't too hopeful about the outcome.

I heard nothing for some time and then she turned up at one of our services. She didn't have to tell me that something wonderful had happened for joy was written over her face. This was her story. She had struggled in prayer for hours and then one night the barrier of bitterness was removed and she was given grace to go to her 'friend' and offer forgiveness. The two embraced and wept and a wonderful feeling of peace flooded her heart while the burden of depression was completely lifted. There was no need to enquire about her mental trouble for she was radiant, having been made whole in the forgiving love of the Lord.

So while we may not be aware of sin in our lives, things happen to us that can cause fear, tension, depression, even bitterness, and these can have a detrimental effect on our health. It's good for us at times to offer the prayer of the Psalmist.

'Search me, O God, and know my heart,
Try me and know my thoughts and see if there be any
evil way in me and lead me in the way everlasting.'

11

Was it Failure?

We live in an age that demands results and expects them right away – indeed the word instant has come to apply to more things than to coffee. This attitude has had a rub-off effect on the Church's ministry of healing. People have said to me, 'Why don't we see immediate healings as in the time of Jesus?' or 'Why aren't all the people you pray for healed?' When Jesus was asked awkward questions He sometimes answered by telling a story or drawing a lesson from the world around Him. In this case I would humbly follow His example and refer to two cases in my experience that may help to answer such questions.

The first concerned a man who lived near Banbridge. One Sunday morning I received a phone call from his daughter who told me that her father, suffering from advanced cancer, was in great pain as drugs seemed to have lost their effect. She requested me to visit him but as it happened I had a pretty full day ahead for in addition to morning worship and a Bible Class there was a special service in the evening. I explained this to her and promised to go first thing on Monday morning. She seemed to understand but I could see that she was disappointed.

After the morning service I returned to the manse, had lunch, and settled down to relax and to prepare for the special occasion in the evening. But as I did so I heard that little voice within which can be so disturbing and it kept saying, 'Go and see that man.' Now I had heard that voice before and I always tried to obey it for when I disobeyed I invariably regretted it. So the matter was decided and right away I rang the family to say that I was on my way.

When I got to the house the father was still in much suffering; his wife and I went to his bedroom and after a chat had a time of prayer and ministry. Nothing dramatic happened and I left him in considerable pain and felt that apart from giving a little comfort, not much had been achieved. However, about half an-hour later the pain suddenly disappeared and a great peace descended not only on the sick man but upon the whole family. Next morning, after a good night's sleep and no return of pain, he said he would like to rise and to sit in the chair at his bedside. He had possessed a good singing voice and as he sat he began to sing hymns which he had learned years before at Sunday School. Two of his favourites were 'God is always near me', and 'What a friend we have in Jesus'. This continued each morning throughout the week and the family began to think that what seemed impossible might happen, their father could be healed. But it was not to be. On Saturday morning he rose as usual and sat in his chair but instead of singing he suddenly slumped and in a few moments was dead.

A cynical person looking on might have said, 'Bringing that minister didn't achieve much for the man died anyway.' And that is exactly what happened but it's not the whole story. About a month after the death I had a visit from the family who told me of what really happened in the home. Their loved one had died without pain and with the peace of the Lord in his heart. The trauma of parting had been greatly eased by the assurance that he had moved to the place where pain and parting are no more; finally all seemed to have experienced a sense of God's presence during those last wonderful days.

On the one hand it could be said that there was failure, in that the father was not restored to health, but on the other hand, what blessing God bestowed upon that family in the time of great need. As I recall that episode, two thoughts come to mind – a Christian, conquering death through the power and love of his Saviour, can never be regarded as failure and secondly, God doesn't always lift the burden but so often gives grace and strength to bear it.

Not long after this I had a rather similar experience. A friend, Rev Andrew Rodgers, minister of Dungannon Church and later Moderator of the General Assembly, rang me with a request to visit a member of his church who had come home from hospital with only a few days to live – he suffered from lung cancer. Having heard the details I expressed the feeling that in this situation my ministry might not achieve very much – I have always guarded against giving people hopes that may not be fulfilled. But you don't put Andrew Rodgers off easily! 'Well', he said, 'this man heard you speak at a meeting in Dungannon and he would like to see you,' and then he added casually, 'of course I'll go for you and take you home again.' As I thought for a moment about this, a very busy minister prepared to give up an afternoon and to drive over 200 miles just to help a sick man, my response was immediate, 'Of course I'll come.'

Now we don't believe that salvation depends on good works but I feel sure that good works will be highly commended in the world beyond. It's not hard to imagine a certain scene in that world and Jesus gives us the setting – it is the Day of Judgement. I see a rather puzzled group who were told by the Lord that they had been accepted into glory because of their love and kindness to Him during their lives on earth. Then I can see someone like Andrew Rodgers stepping forward and saying, 'Lord we don't understand, when did we do these things for You?', and the Lord answers, 'Do you not realize that as you served others, even the lowliest and the least, you were really serving Me?'

We arrived at the home of the sick man in late afternoon. He was in great distress, fighting for every breath. In spite of this he was able to give a little smile and a word of welcome. We prayed with him for some time and there was no change in his condition. I suggested that his doctor should be sent for. Unfortunately he was out on his rounds; efforts were being made to contact him and we were assured that he would come as soon as possible. While we waited it was suggested that oxygen might bring a little ease and Andrew was quick to offer help. He knew where there was a cylinder and also knew how to operate it, so he was off like a flash to get it – typical again of the man!

Again I resorted to prayer, letting my hands rest gently on the sick man's chest in the fervent hope that he might get some relief. After a time I noticed a change in his breathing. It gradually became easier and he fell into a peaceful sleep. Still the breathing became lighter until it faded away and I realised that our friend had passed from the earthly scene.

This was naturally a great shock to me and I wondered what effect it would have on the family but any fears I had were soon dispelled. They had watched their loved one suffer so long that they were relieved to see him at rest and free from pain. The first thing his wife said to me through her tears was, 'God sent you here today to help my husband have a peaceful end.'

Again to the outside world it might appear that our prayer ministry had failed but not so. A few days after the death I received a letter from the mother and signed by the family expressing gratitude for all that was achieved as we prayed together and for the peace that enabled them to say, 'Thy will be done.'

On the way home we discussed the experience at length and were agreed that if we are really in God's will, then He tends to put us in the place where we can best serve Him.

12

Visit to the Holy Land

How would you like to be offered a free trip to the Holy Land, all expenses paid? Most people would be delighted to accept, for this is a part of the world which, for Christian people, is certainly unique. The very thought of walking where Jesus walked, of spending even a short time where he preached and taught, of meeting the kind of people with whom He mingled, such thoughts would bring a yearning to the minds of most of us.

In the early Sixties, visits to the Holy Land had become very popular, especially amongst ministers, indeed to have been there was quite a status symbol! I would have been very keen to go but living in a large and elegant manse in an up-market park, on a church extension salary, made it all out of the question!

Then one day my deaconess, Miss Ella Frank, called at the manse and told me that she had an idea that she would like to discuss with me. It seemed that she had an old friend who was very wealthy and who had learnt late in life that 'there's joy in giving while you're living', so she had decided to give part of her wealth to good causes and sought Miss Frank's guidance in the matter. She, bless her heart, made a suggestion. She thought that a trip to the Holy Land would be a great encouragement to the minister of Dunlop Memorial as he toiled in the building-up of his new congregation! The old lady thought that this was an excellent idea and, of course, when it was put to me there was no delay in accepting. There were, however, two conditions. First of all there must be complete anonymity regarding the donor – I never knew her name – and secondly I was requested to let her have a fairly full account of the tour.

It wasn't hard to agree to these conditions. The matter was quickly settled and I joined a group of local ministers who were planning such a tour the following April. Soon we were making preparations, discussing clothing and equipment and doing some homework on Israel and Jordan. Associating the Holy Land with warm weather we decided that shorts and sandals would be a must – more of this later!

Our party in Jerusalem, 1961.

I kept a pretty full diary during the visit, essential for the requested report, and took lots of photographs, all reminders of a very generous lady and what was indeed the journey of a lifetime. In this brief look-back however, I refer only to a few incidents that remain fresh in my mind, some funny and some serious.

While the tour had been carefully organised we were aware from the start of a certain instability regarding air transport – the firm responsible was Overseas Airways. For example, we had been told that we would break our journey at Athens and that we should do some homework in preparation for a quick tour of that wonderful city. This most of us did, but before setting out from London we were told that there had been a change and that we would now be stopping at Rome. This didn't upset us unduly as we were pleased to have the opportunity of visiting this ancient city, but the signs of poor travel arrangements continued. There were two groups on the plane and next day we flew from Rome to Nicosia in Cyprus. Our party was met by a smaller

A Sheik with an Ulster accent! (A.P.McC)

plane to transport us to Tel Aviv in Israel, while the others were going to Amman in Jordan, but their plane didn't turn up and they had to spend the night in a local hotel. This state of affairs became worse on the homeward journey as we shall see.

On our first morning we were informed that we were going to visit a kibbutz. These communal settlements took different forms and this one happened to be a farming establishment. Their aim was to provide work not only for their own people but especially for the masses of immigrants coming in from all over Europe. These people were glad to find a measure of security and were prepared to undertake any work which they were offered. We saw, for example, a man driving a tractor with a great load of bananas and were told that he was a lawyer who had come from Russia a few weeks earlier.

So we prepared for an interesting day and having equipped ourselves for the heat of the Middle East – shorts etc. as mentioned earlier – we felt we must make use of them right away. When we came down for breakfast, suitably attired as we thought, the young waiter assumed that we were going to play a football match and this we did not dispute! Unfortunately the weather had suddenly turned very cold, quite a few degrees below normal, and when we got to the farmyard which was on an exposed hillside, there was a wind blowing which might well have come all the way from Siberia! We realised that we had misjudged things badly and while the weather became warmer, I don't think the shorts appeared again! When we got back to the hotel the waiter was keen to know if we had won our match, but we reported that it was too cold to play – not entirely an untruth. He was disappointed for us but still seemed to think it was all very funny. He had a great sense of humour and had no trouble in coping with our Irish banter. One evening, for example, the meat at dinner was very tough and someone complained to him about it. 'I'm not surprised, sir,' was his reply, 'it was a very old camel!'

As we travelled around from site to site we came to realise that we were in a country where people were deeply divided, not unlike the situation at home, but the divisions were even more intense. One morning, for example, while staying in Tiberias, I decided to rise early and to go down to the harbour when the fishing boats were returning after a night's fishing on the Sea of Galilee. As I watched this fascinating scene, a woman came along and stopped to look on. Not realising that she was an Arab I simply smiled and said, 'Shalom,' the usual Jewish greeting. Well, she almost screamed at me, 'I don't want to hear Jewish words,' and walked away.

Again when we were leaving Israel to go into Jordan, our bus driver, David, gave us a word of warning. 'Here in Israel,' he said, 'you are safe but over there they think nothing of murder.' When we got through the customs post and set off for our hotel in a taxi, the Arab driver had rather similar words for us, 'You're lucky to have got out of that country alive for they would cut your throat for money.' Sad to say, such attitudes are still very evident amongst the people of the Holy Land – how heart-breaking to the One who was called the Prince of Peace.

If I were to choose highlights from the tour I would put first the sites of the Crucifixion. Unfortunately, there is uncertainty about the authenticity of these sites. The official one is in the Church of the Holy Sepulchre and is certainly very impressive but is rather spoiled by the atmosphere around the tomb. Various branches of the Christian Church control this area and sometimes there is unseemly rivalry. As we stood inside the tomb I noticed a pilgrim, obviously from the East, looking intently at the place where it was alleged the body of Jesus had been placed. As I watched for a moment, a tear trickled down his cheek. Whether the site was authentic or not, here was a man who

John and Anne filming for the BBC.

knew the cost of his salvation.

The other crucifixion site is known as Gordon's Calvary. General Gordon spent several years in Jerusalem towards the end of last century and made a very thorough study of the burial sites. He was quite sure that this was indeed Golgotha with its tomb wherein the body of our Lord had lain. Certainly the official site did not inspire me at all with its noise and gaudiness, but the Garden Tomb was so very different. On our first Sunday at daybreak we worshipped in the Garden near the tomb and it was left to the Irish contingent to conduct the service. It was for us all an unforgettable moment.

Another memorable site was Jacob's Well in Samaria which is believed by scholars to be the authentic place where Jesus talked to the woman. When we arrived at it our guide, an ordained minister of the Church of England, read from St John's Gospel part of the account of the conversation at the well and suddenly the scene came to life and we felt that it was happening before our very eyes. Of course we had a drink of water from the well but no one asked to have the glass refilled! Two young people, Anne and John, were busy taking photographs. They were from the Republic of Ireland and were making a film of the Holy Land for the B.B.C. – it appeared on our T.V. screens the following autumn. Hearing our Northern accents they joined us for a chat. As we left Anne said, 'Isn't it sad that here we can be friendly but at home there are so many barriers.' I've often thought of those words.

Like all good things this wonderful experience all too soon drew to a close and we prepared for the journey home. Through the grapevine we had heard that all was not well with our transport firm and soon our fears were confirmed. We were to leave on Tuesday morning but there was no air transport. We waited, not too patiently all day, and then in the evening a small plane landed, to take us to Athens where we would spend the night, flying home next day. This was disappointing but it meant that we could see something of Athens and have a very pleasant bathe in the 'Med'. But as time went on most people became a little tense and it was quite late before all thirty of us got aboard the small plane – every seat was occupied and the air hostess had to stand. But that was not the worst of her troubles for she had to tell us that there was no food on the plane as it had been stolen. We learnt later the real reason which was that funds apparently were low and shops refused to supply food without cash payment.

We left Athens about 10.00 pm and flew throughout the night, making five stops for fuel. It seemed that there was such a load of passengers that the plane could not take on a full load of fuel – if the passengers weighed heavily it certainly wasn't due to over-eating on the plane!

We arrived in London at 11.00 am having had no sleep and no food since leaving Athens but perhaps more serious were the actual risks of the flight with its frequent landings and take-offs. We were quite unaware of this: the only person in our group who was really scared was an ex-RAF pilot who realised how badly the plane was being handled. Actually, the following September a plane of a similar type – it may have been the same plane – belonging to this company crashed in Norway with thirty schoolboys on board all of whom were killed. That, I think, was the end of this company.

Looking back I can see this visit to the Holy Land as a highlight of my ministry; the Bible came to life in a new way and the reality of our Lord's earthly ministry helped me to understand much better His sublime teaching and His glorious life, death and resurrection.

13

His Ways and Ours

We soon discover in the work of Christian Healing the truth of the words of the prophet Isaiah when he quotes the Lord as saying, 'My thoughts are not your thoughts, neither are your ways My ways.' This applies very much to the results of prayer and ministry. We sometimes feel that certain people should be healed. Those, for example, who have a strong faith and who are living a dedicated life. Just as in the secular world some people receive honours for services to the community, so we are inclined to think that the same thing should apply in the spiritual sphere – that people who give of their best in service to the Kingdom of God should be rewarded in sickness by a gift such as the healing of a disease; while on the other hand we tend to regard people who are outside the Kingdom and who appear to have little interest in spiritual matters as being undeserving of God's healing ministry. Yet it is sometimes the reverse; people who have faith and who are strong witnesses for the Kingdom may not be healed, while wonderful blessings may descend upon the so-called 'unbeliever'. We are all familiar with St Paul's experience, as an example of the former class; he had been specially chosen to proclaim the Gospel in the Gentile world, but there was a snag: he had a 'thorn in the flesh'. He prayed earnestly that it might be removed but his request was not granted. However, on the other hand, I can recall two people who could not have been described as being 'on the Lord's side' and yet they had a wonderful healing experience following prayer ministry.

The first concerned a man in middle life – we will call him Jack – who had been sent home suffering from advanced lung cancer. Nothing more could be done for him in hospital. I first met him at one of our monthly services. At these services a member of our team, a nurse, received people seeking ministry, had a little chat with them regarding their need and then wrote a few words on a card which they could present later to those who would pray with them, thus saving time and sometimes avoiding embarrassing explanations. At one service a healthy looking man came forward and proudly handed me his card on which were the words: 'Had lung cancer'. I have to say that I was completely taken aback for at that time I had never spoken to anyone who had recovered from lung cancer. 'You're a rare one,' I eventually exclaimed, 'Tell us about it.'

It was a fascinating story. Unknown to him he had come home from hospital with only a short time to live. His next door neighbour was a great believer in the power of prayer and being eager to help, asked him if he would be willing to go to a healing service. The reply was brief and to the point. 'I'd go anywhere it I could be cured.' His neighbour wasted no time and brought him to our next service and on the way home afterwards Jack said with great confidence, 'I believe that I have been cured.' And he was. At that time he weighed only seven stones, just half his normal weight, but he began to improve steadily and when he returned to give thanks, six months later, he was back to twelve stones and ready to return to his work. Naturally he was a very happy man and appeared really grateful for all that the Lord had done for him.

It would have been wonderful if I could have reported that Jack had been healed not only physically but also spiritually. This however was not the case. Some two years later I was challenged by a writer in the 'British Weekly' to produce evidence that would convince him that there was really something in what we called 'Divine Healing'. I thought about Jack, hopeful of obtaining possible medical evidence, such as X-rays, that might make some impression on the sceptical journalist. Eventually I was able to contact the neighbour who had brought Jack to our service. I told him what I was looking for. 'Well,' he said, 'I have bad news for you. Jack is 100% fit but is drinking heavily and has deserted his wife.' That was bitterly disappointing to me but what sorrow it must have brought to the heart of the healing Christ. Perhaps this type of person was in the mind of Christ when He said, 'They that are whole need not a physician but they that are sick.' Jesus had a tremendous love for the least and the lost. He had compassion on Jack, a man in his prime. He heard the prayer of His people and healed him physically. Had there been also a spiritual healing that would indeed have been a bonus but the Lord's main concern was that Jack would have another chance to live, and who knows, Jack may yet find abundant life in the Lord.

The other unlikely candidate for Divine Healing was a man – we'll refer to him as Bill – who had severe psoriasis in his right leg. His minister who made the appointment warned me that his language at times could be pretty rough. I assured him that this would not upset me and went ahead and arranged the visit. Well, Bill had been given so much warning about his language that he hardly said a word! He simply pulled up his trouser leg and I have never seen anything quite like it, for you literally could not have put your thumb on a spot where there wasn't psoriasis. Now Bill seemed to think that I had a charm for his disease or perhaps he had heard in Sunday School about Naaman, the leper, who thought that the man of God would simply put his hand on the leprosy and it would disappear. Anyhow I realized that there had to be a fairly long introduction before proceeding to ministry. Bill listened well and seemed to understand what we were about to do. His minister joined me in prayer for healing and afterwards Bill found his tongue and said the right thing as he expressed thanks for the ministry.

This happened on a Friday morning and the following evening Bill retired to bed and having taken off his trousers, got quite a shock for the psoriasis had changed remarkably. Excitedly he called for his wife and when she arrived he simply exclaimed, 'Dammit, Mary, the leg's healed.' And it certainly was. He came to let me see some weeks later and there were still traces of blue on his leg where the psoriasis had been really severe, but it was now completely dead. Unlike the case of Jack, Bill began to go to church from time to time and his minister assured me that there was a slight improvement in his language!

Again we ask the question, 'Why is the Lord so concerned about people like Jack and Bill who, after living for many years in complete indifference to His ways, experience a wonderful blessing, and yet respond in such a disappointing manner?' The only answer I can think of is found in F. W. Faber's greatly loved hymn:

> 'For the love of God is broader
> Than the measure of man's mind;
> And the heart of the Eternal
> Is most wonderfully kind.'

14

Christmas Eve with a Difference

If my life-work were to be assessed by my contribution to debate in the General Assembly I'm afraid I would be found wanting, for apart from occasional reports my only real effort was to put forward a resolution requesting that ministers should be given a week-end off following Christmas. This was passed with great enthusiasm! Unfortunately it came too late for me to benefit from it but down the years I often felt the need of such, following the Christmas rush. As a rule the minister is busy right up to Christmas Eve with possibly a service on Christmas Day, and sometimes before Boxing Day has passed the phone will ring and he will be back on the job!

I can think of one Christmas Eve when this was very much the case. It happened to fall on Sunday evening and as it had been customary to have our Carol Service on the Sunday before Christmas, we could see no good reason why we should change, indeed it was felt by some that this special date might provide a wonderful atmosphere for the Carol singing. There was an excellent congregation, and as singers and readers made their contribution to our worship, we found ourselves being transported back in time to the first Christmas and joining the shepherds and wise men as they presented themselves and their gifts to the Baby Jesus.

As we came toward the end of the service I must confess that I began to feel a sense of relief. All the Christmas parties were over, all the senior members had been visited, all Christmas parcels delivered and in a few minutes the last of the carol services would conclude. I would just have to pronounce the Blessing and then go off to spend a happy Christmas with my family! But it wasn't so simple as that – I just then remembered old Jimmy who was dying with cancer and whom I hadn't seen for some days. I had got to know him not through Church activities but through his illness, for he wasn't what you would call 'Gospel greedy'. A small growth had appeared in his cheek and at first it appeared to be harmless but soon it was found to be malignant. His doctor felt that a course of radium needles could be helpful, but this meant going to the Royal Victoria Hospital in Belfast and neither

Jimmy nor his family had ever been to the city so the question arose as to who would take him to hospital. Jimmy soon solved the problem, 'I'm sure Mr McComb would take me,' was his suggestion! So a few days later he and I set off for the big city. We happened to arrive at the old G.N.R. station at a very busy time. People were either rushing for trains or to work and Jimmy was sure that something terrible had happened. The pace around his farmyard was a lot more leisurely! 'Tell me,' he said, 'is there a fire some place?' I answered him that this was just how people behaved in the city and that all was well!

Eventually we got to hospital and Jimmy started on a course of radium needles. Unfortunately they were not successful and he returned home disappointed but still determined to fight on. At this time there was much talk about a man who lived near Cookstown and who was reputed to have a 'cure' for cancer. Jimmy felt that this could be the answer to his trouble and decided to visit him. His doctor advised him against this and I did likewise but Jimmy was adamant. So one day he and a neighbour set off for Cookstown. The man with the 'cure' was not at home when they arrived and his wife refused to give it to Jimmy, but he was desperate and after much arm-twisting came away with a box of the 'cure'.

On his return no time was wasted in applying the ointment to his cheek with hopes of a complete cure, but it was not to be. The growth was certainly attacked and had the treatment been applied in the very early stages it might have been effective but as it was, only a portion of the growth was cut away leaving quite a mess.

On that Christmas Eve I felt I couldn't go off without having a word with Jimmy who by this time was very weak and suffering a lot of pain. He was lying in a small bedroom off the kitchen, lighted by a little oil lamp. He was really pleased to see me and soon I discovered why. 'Mr McComb', he said, 'you're a brave handy fellow and I think you could do a wee job for me.' He then explained to me that he was in great pain because the dressing on his cheek had not been changed for some time, mainly because his wife just couldn't do it and he was quite sure that I could manage it!

My first reaction was to refuse and to point out that this was a matter for the doctor to attend to, but Jimmy reminded me that having gone against the doctor's orders in going for the 'cure', he felt he couldn't send for him now, certainly not on Christmas Eve. I could see no way out so having washed my hands in a basin in the 'jaw-tub' (the word 'sink' wasn't used in that part of the country), I began the task of removing the dressing. It came away fairly easily but what I saw was not a pretty sight. I didn't look a second time for I never did have a good tummy for that kind of thing, so I quickly applied some of the doctor's ointment on a fresh dressing to the sore and almost immediately he seemed to get a measure of relief.

But I wasn't finished! When I returned to the kitchen, his wife, a good-hearted soul, pointed to the table saying, 'Now it's Christmas Eve and you can't go out without a drop of tea.' On the table was a mug of tea and beside it a plate with a half farl of soda bread well covered with butter and jam. I explained to her that I wasn't really hungry and I never spoke a truer word for the 'wee job' in the bedroom had completely removed my appetite! However, I could see that she would have been hurt if I hadn't partaken of her hospitality, so back to the 'jaw-tub' for a hand wash and somehow I was able to pass myself at the table.

On the way home I couldn't help contrasting the two sets of circumstances which I had just lived through. The lovely Carol service, enabling us to worship again the Child in the Manger, and the minister, clumsily changing a dressing for a dying man in a dingy bedroom. Then I suddenly realised that there was a possible similarity in the two scenes, for the Babe of Bethlehem who received the gifts and worship in that bare stable, became a man and one day He said to His disciples, 'Inasmuch as ye have done it unto the least of these My brethren, ye have done it unto Me.'

Could it be that the Spirit of the Lord so evident in the stable on the first Christmas Eve was also present in that dimly lit bedroom, sharing in the suffering of the dying man and rejoicing in the little act of service that had been shown to him, 'one of the least'.

Anyhow, that episode added much to my happiness over the Christmas Season.

15

A Rare Duet

Most people like to get something for nothing. The business world is well aware of this and almost every morning in our junk mail there will be the offer of free gifts. Usually there is a string attached, we have to purchase something before that gift becomes ours, but sometimes we are told that even if we don't buy anything, the gift will be ours to keep and that offer is hard to resist!

I am reminded of one such offer made to me many years ago, for which I fell. During my spell in Armagh I belonged to a small group of young men who had a lot in common, we were all unmarried, hadn't much money to spend and were fond of music. The organist in the cathedral, Duncan Peel, was a member of the group and was very keen on good voice production both on the platform and in the pulpit. He was quite sure that singing was excellent for improving this and went so far as to make an offer to another member of our group, a local curate, and myself. He would be prepared to give us a few singing lessons and there would be no fees.

Well, that was an offer too good to miss and we both agreed to accept. Right away Duncan arranged times when we could go to his home for lessons. After my third or fourth lesson, he asked me rather absentmindedly if I had as yet sung in public. I was somewhat taken aback, 'Sing in public,' I said, 'I should think not.' 'Oh,' he replied, 'awful people sing in public.' I don't think lessons continued long after that but I didn't realise how soon his rather rash statement was to become a reality!

And this is how it happened. My friend John, whose surname was Mark (as in the book of Acts), and I were approached by a minister, Rev Tom Barry, who had two small congregations just over the border in Co Monaghan. He invited us to help at a concert which was to be held shortly. Life for him was a real struggle and if something unforeseen arose, say a leak in the church roof, Tom had to resort to sales, concerts etc. to help meet the cost of repairs. We felt we must help in any way we could although we were well aware of difficulties. It was the dead of winter, the roads were bad and we weren't familiar with that part of the country. However, we promised to go and were told that we could speak for fifteen minutes on any subject of our choosing and that a few good 'stories' would also be appreciated.

After taking a number of wrong turns we eventually got to the hall where the concert was to be held, just on this side of the Border. It had been well advertised; over a wide area it had been made known that a popular concert party from Portadown would be responsible for the programme. We were told that people had come from Keady, Castleblaney, Newtownhamilton and surrounding districts to hear this great concert party.

Tom had reserved seats for us at the front and everything seemed set for a great night's entertainment. Then came the shattering news; apparently there was very bad fog around Portadown and the concert party felt that in such circumstances it would be quite impossible to make the long journey to the concert hall.

Well, the result on Tom was predictable. Somewhat tense at the best of times, he almost went to pieces on hearing this news and no wonder, a hall filled with people who had paid their half-crown or whatever and no programme. But Tom quickly recovered and had a brainwave. In an audience like this there must be a lot of talent – let's have a D.I.Y. effort!

It seemed to be the only option and so he went around with pencil and paper writing down the names of all who could do something – sing, recite, tell jokes or play the piano. Eventually he came to us. 'You two boys will sing,' he said. I right away refused, but John, big-hearted as usual, felt we must play our part and in the end persuaded me to join him.

Now I knew that John could whistle, indeed he was a very good whistler but I had never heard him sing. However, when it was announced that the two visiting ministers were going to sing a duet, the applause was tremendous – they knew they were on to a good thing. At that stage we weren't even quite sure what we were going to sing but John felt that 'Galway Bay', very popular at that time, might see us through. So we began to sing and the audience, bless them, joined in perhaps realising that we could do with support. This suited us fine and with plenty of people taking part we were able to lead the singing and what might have been a fiasco turned out a great success. But there was no demand for an encore!

However, the story didn't end there. Some years afterwards I was conducting an evening service in Legacurry Church near Lisburn and afterwards a lady came to speak to me in the vestry. She belonged to Tom Barry's church in Co Monaghan where I had preached several times. 'I remember,' she said, 'you coming down to our country.' Of course I thought she might have remembered a sermon or something I had said, but no, 'I remember,' she said, 'the night that you and Mr Mark sang 'Galway Bay'.' John has gone to Glory but I know he would have enjoyed that remark!

16

A One Off?

One thing we have always guarded against in the Church's Ministry of Healing, is giving people hopes and assurances that may not be fulfilled. Much harm has been done in this ministry by people, usually outside the church, who sometimes, following prayer and the laying-on of hands, will assure patients that they have been completely healed. A few days later it may be discovered that this is not so, and the result is that the local minister and perhaps also the doctor will have to attempt to put right the damage that has been done to all concerned. We must always remember that God alone can foretell the future and we are very happy to leave it in His hands.

However, there is a promise that we can make; it has been our experience in almost every case when a person receives ministry that a blessing follows. You see we impress on those seeking help and healing that they are coming not just to a minister or to a church healing service but to Christ Himself, and He does not disappoint but is eager and willing to bless. The blessing may take different forms. There can be instant healing and while this is rare it is wonderful to witness. Or there may be healing extended over quite a long period and requiring on-going prayer support. Or there may be no physical healing at all but the blessing may come through an easing of pain. Finally, it may be a blessing of deep inward peace and strength to keep on top of the disease.

Even after stating this approach I hesitate to relate the following account of a person suffering from M.S. whom we shall call Bill. I have ministered to a number of people suffering from this dread disease, for which there is, as yet, no cure, but steady progress in research brings one nearer. Some certainly have been helped physically and spiritually through prayer ministry but in one case only in my experience has there been what appears to be a cure.

Bill's ministry began on a lovely summer evening and continued for just over a year. It was the stark contrast of that evening that so impressed the scene on my mind. We were surrounded by flowers and shrubs, bird song and a glorious sunset; and then into those idyllic surroundings came Bill, a young man in his early thirties and yet because of M.S. he was unable to walk the few yards from his car to the front door – his wife and I had almost to carry him inside.

I was given a full account of the progress of his disease over almost ten years, in which he had no remission but unrelenting decline. He knew little about prayer and the healing ministry, but he had a powerful desire to become well again. I talked to him for a long time explaining what was involved in this ministry and that it could mean a long and demanding process, but he was quite prepared, as was his wife, to undertake it.

Well, he came every month for the remainder of the year. It was made easy for both of us in this way: at almost every visit he was able to report progress, however small. I can remember him walking proudly with two sticks, then with one and finally, wonder of wonders, walking from his car completely unaided. 'Yes,' said Bill, 'I sent the sticks back to my friend that I borrowed them from. I don't need them any longer!' He continued to come occasionally until he had been restored to normal health again.

I should point out that they had been married for some ten years but because of Bill's disease decided that it would be better not to have a family. Now the situation had changed. One evening they came to see me and they were really full of the joy of living. Bill had got his old job back, they had been offered a house with the option of buying and best of all, with a lovely smile his wife said, 'I'm pregnant and if it's a wee boy we're going to call him Andrew!' What an occasion of rejoicing and thanksgiving.

The baby duly arrived, a strong healthy wee boy and he was called Andrew. They brought him several times to our home and like most wee boys, even those called Andrew, he was quite a handful!

Bill was a keen photographer and was able to resume his side-line, wedding photography, something that requires a steady hand and a cool head. As an expression of gratitude for my help, he suggested photographing our home, the lovely old manse of First Dromara. I pointed out to him that the house faced sou'-east and that the best time to take photos would be in the morning. So shortly after this, one sunny morning about 7 o'clock the doorbell rang. That happened at such an early hour usually in the case of a death in the congregation or if someone were seriously ill. I rushed downstairs in my dressing-gown and opened the door and found Bill on the doorstep equipped with a very large camera. When I mentioned the morning for photography I

Photograph of First Dromara Manse taken by Bill at around 7.00 am!

certainly hadn't thought of 7.00 am! Well, he carried that heavy camera around the house photographing it from many angles – the resulting photographs were excellent. But one thought kept recurring in my mind as I watched him at work – what a contrast to his first visit to the manse!

We kept in touch for several years but gradually we lost contact. At our last meeting, Andrew was about to start school and Bill was living a very full and active life.

Would that I could say this about all the M.S. patients to whom I have ministered but even if, for the others, the burden of weakness and frustration can be eased a little, it is surely worthwhile.

17

Over the Border

Most of us are familiar with the crack about the couple who had invited friends for supper. It was a pleasant occasion but as sometimes happens, the friends stayed much longer than was anticipated and eventually the husband losing his patience, said to his wife, 'I think dear, we should go to bed and let these people get away home!' I'm sure we've all had experience of guests like that, good friendly people but just outstaying their welcome.

We had a friend of that type in the early Armagh days, Rev Grant Smith, a bachelor and a rather lonely person. He would arrive for tea around 5.00 pm and inform us that he was looking forward to a good night's chat as his taxi wouldn't be calling for him until 11.00 pm! It was always a long evening but one good thing was that Grant had the knack of considering an episode or a situation from four or five different angles and this helped to put the time in! There was one difficulty, however, in all this. While Grant enjoyed our hospitality, he was unable to return it. He had a housekeeper who did a very good job but drew the line at entertaining his friends. So, keenly aware of his indebtedness to us, he had to find some other way of showing his gratitude, and he came up with this. We would all go to Dublin for a couple of days and he would be responsible for 'bed and breakfast'.

So one lovely morning in May 1948 we set off for Dublin, Grant in the back seat passing his usual pithy comments on the outside world. We arrived at the hotel which he had booked, not a five star one but quite comfortable. I must point out that as well as repaying our hospitality, Grant had another reason for going to Dublin. In those days many war restrictions still continued, for example it wasn't possible for men to buy elastic braces, they had to be content with the non-stretch type. Most men were able to manage but Grant was small and very stout – of him it could certainly be said that the trouble wasn't his Billy Bunter girth, he just wasn't tall enough for his weight! The result of this was that sometimes when he stooped there would be an ominous sound and off would fly the back buttons of his trousers, and, of course, not being married there was no one to sew them on again!

So on the first morning after our arrival we headed right away for a shop that sold elastic braces. Now if we left the North in brilliant sunshine, it was quite different in Dublin – a steady downpour all day. Unfortunately I hadn't brought a hat and not being blessed with a lot of 'thatch', realised that if we were to get around in the rain I would have to buy one. In view of what happened the next day I should point out that hats were not rationed in the North and so there was no long-term advantage in buying one in Dublin. The short-term advantage was some shelter from the constant downpour.

In the shop Grant was delighted to get what he dearly longed for – a pair of stretching braces – but now a problem arose. Grant could certainly not have been regarded as a 'hard-liner' concerning church doctrine; indeed a story went the rounds about an old lady in his congregation who said, 'We've got a great wee minister in our Church now, for sometimes in his sermon it's 'no hell' and another Sunday he gives us a queer dose of it!' The latter case may have been when he was attacking smuggling. Around the border area at that time, smuggling was a popular pastime and quite a few of Grant's congregation may have been involved in some form of it, so his condemnation required a lot of courage. As he was indeed a person of principle and having attacked smuggling in the pulpit he felt he couldn't be party to it even though it concerned only a pair of braces! He asked the shop assistant how he could get the braces over the border. Would it mean that he would have to get an export licence? The young man laughed and said, 'Not at all, just wear them.' But Grant had other ideas.

So after a pleasant break we headed for home and arrived at the border. Some time earlier a car, driven by a lady, had been found to be carrying quite a load of contraband goods, cigarettes, liquor, silk stockings etc. The customs men felt that the answer was to confiscate the outfit, car and all, with the result that the lady had to look for a lift home. After that 'take' the men were on their toes, perhaps looking for another big haul as they put to us the usual question, 'Anything to declare?' 'Yes,' said Grant as he produced the braces. Now I think they may have regarded the braces as a kind of red herring with the result that they went through our car with a fine comb. We were made to get out while they examined our bags, opened bonnet and boot and even looked below the body. Of course they found nothing but one thing, my new hat! I explained to them about the heavy rain on the previous day, but they weren't in the mood to listen.

They took hat and braces to their office where I received a receipt for both and was told that if I applied to Dublin Castle they might be sent to someone in the Republic. I felt rather sore about the hat for I didn't really need a new one and anyway I could probably have bought it cheaper and better in the North. I later applied to Dublin Castle giving the name of a friend in County Monaghan who like myself had a rather big head! It was sent to him some weeks later stuffed into a large envelope and, of course, completely ruined. But Grant never made any attempt to retrieve his braces and this to him was a big loss as for many more months he had to put up with the losing of his trouser buttons! Perhaps he got this remarkable spirit from his father who had been left a sizeable legacy by an uncle, but when he discovered that all the capital had been invested in Guinness shares, wouldn't touch a penny of it.

Now that attitude may seem silly to some people but I feel that we should respect those who take a stand on principle, knowing that sacrifices may be involved, whether it be concerning a legacy or just a pair of elastic braces!

18

Christ is the Healer

By the early Seventies Belfast was presenting to the outside world an image of violence and hate. It was being seen as a city torn apart by sectarian strife and religious bigotry. In such a situation it seemed very unwise to expect people from overseas to come here for a conference and yet that was just what we in the Churches' Council of Healing were contemplating. We discussed the possibility at length, prayed much about it and finally decided to go ahead with the holding of an international conference under the title, 'Christ is the Healer', the venue being Stranmillis Training College and the time September 1976. It was a risky undertaking and some had the fear that it would be a flop but we felt that it was in God's Will and that it would not fail.

I happened to be honorary secretary of the Council at this time and while responsible for a lot of the spade work, had the privilege of meeting a number of very interesting and dedicated people. Some came from faraway places, Canada, U.S.A.. Australia and, of course, from all parts of the British Isles, especially from the Republic where there was a growing interest in the Healing Ministry mainly because of the influence of the Charismatic Movement. Eighty-four members lived in the College while about two hundred were non-residential. From the start everything went well. The visitors seemed surprised and delighted to find themselves in such a peaceful atmosphere – they probably expected street fighting and the sound of bombs exploding!

We had organised a pretty full programme with mornings and evenings fully booked, while in the afternoons a number of tours were available, the one through the Shankill and Falls being especially popular. Most of the speakers came from the mainland, complemented by a few of our own 'specialists' and almost every aspect of the Healing Ministry was covered with due appreciation of the great work being done by the Medical Profession. There was also much concern expressed about the healing of the community. It lasted four full days and each morning a leader of one of the main denominations brought greetings and the assurance of prayers and good

Members of the Executive Committee.

wishes. The Chairman of the Council, Rev Fred Baillie presided at most meetings and helped to create a wonderful spirit of togetherness.

While I have forgotten much of what was put across during the conference one or two little episodes are still fresh in my mind. The first took place in St Anne's Cathedral on the Thursday evening. To conclude the conference we had planned a great healing service in the Cathedral when the various churches would be represented as prayers were offered for the sick and for our community, with the laying-on of hands for those in need. An excellent sermon was preached by Dr Hedley Plunkett.

Before the service I happened to be speaking to the Dean – Samuel Crooks, the first 'black Santa', who seemed surprised that I wasn't taking part. I pointed out to him that we were giving preference to our visitors while we stayed in the background. But Sammy, as we affectionately knew him, did not accept my explanation and, with his tendency to call a spade a spade, replied, 'You've been in the background all week organising things, it's time you got some limelight!' I explained to him that I just couldn't take part as I hadn't my robes, to which he replied, 'We'll soon settle that.' Away he went to his vestry and came back with a bright blue cassock – he seemed to think that blue was the appropriate colour for a Presbyterian! It fitted perfectly and soon I found myself processing with the others, my simple cassock getting me through very well.

After the service those taking part mingled with the large congregation. It was estimated that about four hundred were present and we learnt that many had been blessed in body and in spirit.

While we chatted I was approached by a nun who asked me to pray for her. In conversation I discovered that she had been involved in the 'Women for Peace' movement, had received a lot of criticism from certain unexpected quarters and was in great need of spiritual help. I gladly agreed to her request and she knelt on the cathedral floor while I placed my hands on her shoulders and prayed that she might be released from her anxiety and depression. She was most grateful and seemed to feel that a burden had been lifted from her mind. I was later very amused as I thought how unusual it all was – a Presbyterian minister wearing an Anglican cassock, praying for a Roman Catholic nun in a Church of Ireland cathedral! While I have never been deeply involved in the ecumenical movement I felt that this was an episode that would have merited its blessing! But not far from the cathedral that night things were very different as the violence continued.

On the following morning before people set off for home we had a kind of open forum where members were invited to comment on the conference or to share any relevant thoughts. In the group from Dublin there was a priest, a small man but with a big heart, who seemed to be filled with the joy of the Lord. It wasn't long until he found his way to the platform and right away made a strange request. He wanted two Presbyterian ladies to join him. In a moment two rather tall ladies were at his side and he linked arms with them – what a rare sight, this little priest supported by two biggish Presbyterian ladies! He went on to explain the reason for all this. Some years before he had read a book entitled 'I believe in Miracles' by Kathryn Kuhlman. He had also heard of remarkable happenings at her meetings which he found hard to believe. After much thought he decided to go to Pittsburgh where she ministered, to find out for himself.

At the meeting which he attended Kathryn Kuhlman referred to her recent visit to the Pope and this for him was the last straw. For the Pope to receive a woman evangelist was just unthinkable. When he returned to his hotel he wrote a letter to Kathryn Kuhlman asking if she was really honest regarding her reported reception by the Pope and stating that, if possible, he would like

Delegates from our Council who attended a 'follow-up' conference in Edinburgh.

to meet her. She did not arrange a meeting with him but instead sent one of her workers who happened to be a Presbyterian and who brought with her a photo of Kathryn Kuhlman being received by the Pope! That really shook this little priest and he began to see things differently. They talked together for a long time and before his visitor left he came to know Christ as Saviour and Lord, and his life had been changed. He told that in his earlier days he didn't like Presbyterians and that was putting it mildly, but since that evening in Pittsburgh his attitude towards them had completely changed and that was why he was so pleased to testify standing between two Presbyterian friends.

He finished with a remark which brought much joy to us, the organisers. He said that he had come to a conference on Divine Healing but for him it had been something more, it had been a healing conference. We knew that others had had a similar experience making us feel that it had all been well worthwhile.

19

When People Pray

Those of us who watch rugby matches on television will hear the commentator occasionally refer to the boiler-house', the place in the scrum where the really strong men are the main source of power. In Dunlop Memorial we had what was known as the Prayer Healing Group, consisting of ten or twelve members who had a strong personal belief in the power of prayer. I tended to regard it as 'the boilerhouse' – a wonderful source of strength for the entire work of the congregation and especially for the sick. It was a great comfort to those who were very ill, perhaps terminally ill, and to others facing operations or experiencing bereavement, just to know that they were remembered by folk at the church.

One evening a member arrived looking very worried and we soon discovered the reason for his concern. His wife, who was pregnant, had been to hospital the previous day and after tests it was discovered that there was a high sugar content in her blood. She was told to come back in a fortnight and that if there was no improvement in her condition she would have to come to hospital and be confined to bed for the remainder of the pregnancy – three months. This was serious news for the family for not only was there concern about the mother but there was also a problem inside the home where there were two small children with the father as the sole wage earner.

We sought God's help in this distressing situation praying for each member of the family. This was repeated the following week and a few days later the mother returned to hospital for the usual tests. The first test was taken by a nurse who knew the case and the results of previous testing. To her surprise it proved to be negative. Just to be sure it was repeated with the same result. The nurse was really puzzled and felt that she should have a second opinion and sent for the ward doctor. He had a good look at the previous results and then made a thorough test himself: Again it proved negative and this he reported to the expectant mother and then to her surprise he said, 'Do you believe in prayer?' 'Yes,' she said, 'and a group in my church have been praying for me.' 'Well,' said the young doctor, 'that explains it for nothing

Pamela

else could.' And off he went while the mother returned home and was able to stay there until the baby was due. Whether our prayers were responsible for this amazing outcome or not I cannot say, but I know that there was much rejoicing in our group when the father came with the news.

I think of another case when remarkable things happened following earnest prayer – this time in my retirement. One Monday morning I received a phone call from a young man whose little daughter. Pamela, was in the Children's Hospital, suffering from leukaemia. He asked me to call sometime to minister to her, and not regarding it as a matter of urgency I promised to call toward the end of the week. However, a short time later he rang again to tell me that the doctors had spoken to him and his wife, explaining that as well as leukaemia, Pamela was suffering from pneumonia which prevented treatment for leukaemia and this was urgently required. They broke the news gently to the parents – unless the pneumonia could be checked fairly quickly, the child had only a few days to live.

The father was naturally shattered. I could sense his desperation over the phone. 'If I come down for you, could you come right away?' In a case like this one doesn't hesitate and in less than one hour he had picked me up and we were on our way to hospital. Never have I had such a fast drive to the city!

At the hospital we found the little side room full of people, friends and relatives, all very concerned. Pamela was seriously ill and in a very nervous state – a stranger going near her cot really upset her. It seemed that a normal prayer ministry would not be possible. I discussed the matter with her minister, Rev Stuart Finlay of Annalong who had joined us and we decided to have a prayer tryst for Pamela that night at eleven o'clock. After a moment of prayer not only for the child but also that the burden of anxiety might be lifted from the hearts of the loved ones we returned to our homes. Stuart decided to increase the number of prayers and rang up a few of his members whom he thought would be willing to help, inviting them to come to the Church Hall at 11.00 pm. Many others I know were involved in the prayer vigil, but perhaps the greatest response was at Annalong where between thirty and forty people turned up at the set time to pray for Pamela.

The next morning there was no real change in her condition, doctors had done everything possible and they could only wait and hope that the pneumonia would very soon abate. For most of the day the position remained critical and unchanged but by late evening there was a remarkable turn for the better which continued throughout the night and by Wednesday afternoon all traces of pneumonia had disappeared. Shortly after, the doctors were able to resume the vital treatment for leukaemia. Pamela responded very well and is now a healthy teenager. She came to see me shortly after returning from hospital and, sitting on my knee, told me some of the things that had recently happened to her. For one thing most of her hair had come out due to treatment and I could see her looking intently at my head. Then she whispered 'You haven't got much hair either!'

It could, of course, be said that in both cases what happened might have been a matter of coincidence and I accept that, but down the years I have noted that 'coincidences' tend to happen more often when people pray!

20

Marriage Vows are for the Keeping

Anniversaries are usually times of celebration when we rejoice and give thanks for happy memories and those who helped to provide them for us. They can also be occasions for taking stock, considering the way we have travelled in the past, with perhaps a look towards the future.

On my tenth anniversary as minister of First Dromara, I was looking through various records of church activities that had taken place during these ten years and in particular the marriage books. I discovered that no less than thirty-one couples had been married during that period; I was in touch with a good number of them but others had moved from our district and I knew little about them. I wondered how all these marriages had turned out and the idea came to me of a get-together when we could all meet again, renewing the bond of friendship and exchanging news and gossip. The idea was well received by everyone and the wives of elders and committee members gladly undertook to provide supper on this very special occasion.

Perhaps the most difficult part of the venture was to contact all these couples, especially those living far afield, but with the help of friends and relations we managed to collect all the addresses. We weren't at all sure how they would respond but to our delight, twenty-nine couples accepted our invitation – the others had genuine reasons for being unable to attend. It was almost too much to expect all fifty-eight partners to turn up as arrangements can so easily be upset even at the last minute, but turn up they did, all fifty-eight of them! In days when broken marriages were becoming almost commonplace, it was a great joy for us to note that in the marriages celebrated during those ten years, the bonds were still intact.

We hadn't planned a programme for the occasion as we knew that there would be so much to talk about that any further entertainment would be unnecessary; from the start there was a loud and steady hum of conversation. 'Where are you living now?' 'Have you a family'?' 'What is your job?' These and many others were the questions put and answered. Then we had a break for supper and our womenfolk made it a very special meal.

But perhaps the highlight of the evening came afterwards when we invited Dr Howard Cromie to give a short address on 'The make-up of a happy marriage'. Howard was well qualified for this task for he and his dear wife Kathleen, have set us a wonderful example of a successful marriage and a happy home based on sound Christian principles. Towards the end of the helpful address he shared with us his ten commandments for a happy marriage. Some of these I can recall and Howard has kindly permitted me to use them in this article. They were originally delivered in the language of the Authorised Version of the Bible but in keeping with modern trends I have changed them to the wording of today:

- You should work hard to ensure that your marriage is a success – the things worth having in life are usually costly.
- You should not expect too much of your partner – you married a human being, not an Archangel.
- You should be quick to show appreciation to your partner – a word of thanks can go a long way.
- You should look after your finances carefully – failure to live within your means can be the road to ruin.
- You should be kind to your in-laws! – mothers-in-law sometimes get a bad press but where would we be without them?
- Be faithful to your partner and your marriage will be blessed – where there is fidelity there will be no grounds for suspicion.

The sum of all the commandments is this: You should love the Lord your God above all, and your partner as yourself;

On this high note the evening drew to a close but many stayed on to chat and to share experiences. It seemed to have been an enjoyable occasion for all but there was more to it than that. A number spoke to me in appreciation of the church's interest in them and their matrimonial affairs. One man said quite openly that while his marriage was not on the rocks, he had been made to realise during the evening that seeds of trouble had been appearing from time to time and he was now determined to put things right.

This happened almost twenty years ago. I have lost touch with most of the couples but I've got a feeling that many of them are maintaining their marriage vows and living happily ever after! Christian civilisation, which we sometimes take for granted, is built on a number of very important foundations. One of them is the keeping of marriage vows and the maintenance of a happy Christian home. Where this is neglected the whole fabric of society can be in danger of collapse. Our Church in recent years has established an excellent system of marriage counselling – many marriages have been saved from falling apart and consequently little children spared heart-break and confusion.

If I might finish on a personal note, having happily passed the fifty year milestone on the wedded way, I would express my feelings in a little story which I have sometimes told at wedding receptions. It tells of a young French lady who came to visit London. Hailing a taxi, she told the driver that she wished to be driven to Buckingham Palace. Westminster Abbey and St. Paul's Cathedral. In broken English she asked the driver what this would cost and the reply was, 'Seven pounds.' The taxi-man did his job well and brought her back to her hotel. Again she enquired about the cost and this time the reply was: 'A tenner will do.' However, the visitor from France was not so easily fooled. 'Non non,' she said, 'you are dearer to me than when we were engaged.'

When a couple, with many years of married life behind them, can look across the breakfast table and say to their partner as many of us could, 'Darling, you are dearer to me than when we were engaged,' there you have the hallmark of a really happy marriage!

21

A Friend in Need

The year 1978 began during a spell of very severe frost, the worst for many years with night temperatures plummeting to minus 10°C and during the day remaining below zero. Soon reports were coming in of frozen pipes and homes without heat. In the manse we had kept the central heating system just 'ticking over' throughout the night and had escaped trouble. But on Wednesday 3rd January things were getting worse. I became concerned about a number of our people especially old folk living alone, and decided to call with a few of them. Most were coping quite well but in one case this was not so – an elderly lady living alone in a large house. Her heat was supplied by a cooker but as the inlet pipe to the tank was frozen, no water was available and so the cooker could not be lighted. The mains water supply was still available but the problem was to get it from the tap to the tank on the second floor. After searching around for quite a time I found a length of garden hose which was long enough to do the job and in a few minutes water was pouring into the tank and soon it was safe to light the cooker.

By this time I felt like a meal and headed for home with that feeling of satisfaction that comes when you have made even a little contribution to someone's well-being. But this feeling was short lived. When I arrived at the manse I found my wife very upset. A neighbour in Newcastle had telephoned to say that water was trickling from the eaves of our bungalow, later to be our retirement home, and that we should come as soon as possible. Unfortunately, Queenie had no idea where I was and so was unable to contact me – no car phones in those days! However, she wisely got in touch with Lindsay Graham and explained the position – he was our estate agent.

There was no time for a proper meal – just a cup of tea and a sandwich and we were on the road to Newcastle. Along the road we realised what had probably happened. The bungalow had been let to a teacher for the winter who, going off for the Christmas holidays had forgotten to turn off the water supply; it later proved that this was exactly the case.

When we got to 'Shalom' – the name given to our bungalow and which means Peace – it seemed very inappropriate that night! There was very little light inside as the flooding had cut off electric power and, of course, there was no heat. However, before the night was over the old saying 'a friend in need is a friend indeed' took on new meaning for us. Lindsay Graham and Bertie Hanna, an elder from our local church, had done an excellent job and were in process of getting things under control. In the lounge there was a steady stream of water coming through the central light fitting with the result that about an inch of water covered the carpet. Our friends had been able to obtain a large drum which was placed under the 'leak' from the roof space, thus preventing further damage to the carpet. But now that we had arrived they left with our heart-felt thanks for all their help.

However, our work wasn't quite over; water was still coming in steadily through the lounge ceiling. This meant that the roof space must be flooded, which at that time had not been floored. I decided to have a look and what I saw was a depressing sight. The space between rafters was covered with quite a layer of water.

We had two options. We could simply forget about the situation in the attic, head for home and come back next morning to find that the lounge ceiling had collapsed and was lying on top of the saturated carpet, or we could attempt to soak up the water. Reluctantly we chose the latter course. This meant gathering up sponges, towels, clothes, anything that would hold water, with basins and buckets to wring them into, and with the help of a torch to start the job of soaking up. I don't know what the temperature was outside but in the roof-space it felt like the North Pole! The job, at first, seemed beyond us but in less than two hours it was accomplished and all the water had been soaked up.

As I thought about this tough assignment afterwards, I was reminded of a childhood experience. Sometimes when things were busy on the farm, the 'weans' would be called in to help with the thinning of the turnip crop – an awful job, perhaps one of the things that put me off being a farmer! To get down on one's knees at the end of a drill on a hot day in June, and to look at the other end of the drill, possibly 150 yards away and to know that you had to crawl all that distance, thinning all the way, was indeed a daunting prospect! At the present time the authorities seem to have difficulty in knowing how to punish evildoers. I suggest that a week of turnip-thinning would deter even the hardened criminal! However, even in my brief experience of this work, I learnt an important lesson – instead of keeping your eye on the length of the drill, it is better to concentrate on the few inches where you are working. This had got me through many an irksome task and was certainly useful in the roof-space on that bitterly cold night.

But we don't have to end on a gloomy note. Just shortly after our job was finished, the doorbell rang and our neighbour, Mrs McKibben, was there with an invitation to come to her home for a cup of tea. The writer of the Epistle to the Hebrews tells us to be careful when we have folk in our home lest we should be entertaining angels unawares. In no way could anyone have mistaken us for angels as we emerged from our ordeal, but our neighbour played the angelic part extremely well. Soon we were seated at a blazing fire, enjoying hot scones, sandwiches etc. I have been fortunate down the years to partake of many an excellent meal but I doubt if I ever enjoyed one more than on that occasion! As we came away, the world around us seemed to have changed, the frost was less severe and the water damage really nothing to worry about!

Perhaps our inner glow was in some ways akin to the experience of the shepherds as they left the stable to return to their sheep – the Love of the Christ Child had warmed their hearts. That love expressed through His followers can have the same affect today. In a world that so often seems cold and loveless, let us strive to be channels of His friendship, His compassion, His love.

22

Dry Bones

In the book of Ezekiel there is an account of the prophet's strange vision in 'the valley of dry bones'. He was carried in the Spirit of the Lord to a valley which was full of bones, and the Spirit said to him, 'Son of man, can these bones live?' His reply was, 'O Lord Thou knowest.' He was then told to proclaim to the bones that they would be restored to life; this he did and eventually the bones became a great army. We need not consider the interpretation of this vision but simply point out that its aim would seem to have been to make clear that God can intervene in the affairs of the everyday, achieving what would seem to be impossible.

I remember considering this vision in relation to the Ministry of Divine Healing and the question arising, 'Could bones be affected by prayer?' I didn't have to wait very long until I had an opportunity of attempting to answer it. In my congregation was an ex-serviceman who had come through the horrors of Dunkirk. He was struck in the thigh by shrapnel during the retreat and really was a case for hospital but he realised that this would mean becoming a prisoner of war, so he decided to struggle on. He made it alright but at a price – serious damage had been done to his leg.

The condition became worse and some years later not only was he suffering a lot of pain but also walking had become very difficult. He attended hospital once a month and while all efforts were made to ease his pain, it was pointed out to him that the necessary plate could not be inserted in his leg until the bone had ceased to deteriorate, and the hope that this would happen was not very high. So each month the femur was measured and always the same result: 'further deterioration'. He had become very depressed feeling that his active life was almost over. In this mood he came to me and enquired about the healing ministry in our church. 'Do you think that my condition could be helped by prayer'?' I reminded him of the words of Jesus. 'All things are possible to him that believeth'. I don't think he was a strong believer' and certainly my faith in this instance was not all that it should have been. However, we worked out a plan – I would minister to him in his home every fortnight and the members of our prayer-healing group would pray earnestly for him every week. This seemed to be a happy and helpful arrangement and it continued for several months but without visible results. After the monthly measurement of the bone came the depressing result: 'further slight deterioration'.

Then one afternoon I received a phone call from our friend who was very excited. He had been to hospital and after the usual examination had been told that for the first time the condition of the bone was static. The surgeon concerned was naturally cautious but said that if this condition continued for at least a further two months, they would consider surgery with the hope that a plate could he implanted. This was wonderful news and certainly encouraged us in our praying. At the end of two months doctors were satisfied that the condition was static and went ahead with the operation. They did a wonderful job and in a few weeks' time the patient was able to walk with the aid of a stick and eventually managed very well without one.

Apart from helping to build up my faith in the power of Christ 'to heal all manner of diseases' as stated in the Gospels, this case seemed to me to be a notable example of how medical skill and prayer can work together to achieve a remarkable healing.

Another case of bone healing occurred some years later. A young woman sought prayer ministry for her left leg that had shortened as a result of a car accident. Her shinbone had been shattered and after careful surgery, had been restored but with two unavoidable results – a shortening of the leg which meant wearing a heavily built-up shoe, and quite a big lump on her shin. Again my faith was tested. I wondered how on earth prayer ministry could have any effect on this condition.

We discussed the matter at length and as I talked to her I realised that she had thought much about the matter and I was reminded of the case of Paul and the cripple in Lystra. Paul felt that the cripple had faith to be healed. This woman seemed to have that kind of faith and after prayer, an amazing thing happened. She almost jumped from her chair and walked around the room saying, 'I've got a spring in my foot – I've got a spring in my foot.' It seemed that she had trouble putting her foot down and when it did touch the floor it tended to spring up. She also had a strange but not unpleasant feeling in her leg around the area of the fracture which she described as 'pins and needles'. These sensations continued until she went to bed. After a good night's sleep she woke up and the first thing she did after dressing was to try on a normal shoe instead of the built-up one. To her delight she was able to walk without the slightest limp, which meant that the leg had been restored to its normal length. In addition the lump on her shinbone was a little smaller. She went off to the school where she taught with a song in her heart and later in the morning put on 'Wellies' and took her class for a two mile nature walk, a thing she hadn't done for a very long time. About a month after this she called with me wearing ordinary shoes, walking perfectly and the lump on her leg still there but much smaller.

Like Thomas I would tend to have doubts and sometimes I have to see results before I am fully convinced; in this case, I think even that doubting disciple would have exclaimed, 'It is indeed the work of my Lord, the risen Christ.'

23

Fellowship

Fellowship was very important in the Early Church; the word 'Koinonia' which occurs in the book of Acts was applied to the followers of Jesus and simply means 'Christian Fellowship'. It is still important today and one of the encouraging features of modern church life is the new emphasis that is being placed upon the need for Christian people to meet for fellowship in addition to the weekly diet of worship. While church members need this fellowship it is even more essential for ministers. The ministry can be a lonely life even with the blessing of a happy home to support one. Whilst various men's clubs and associations are open to ministers, they don't as a rule feel quite at home in such, realising that they are regarded, because of their role and calling, as being somewhat different from the others.

Probus, a club movement which has grown in popularity in recent years, tries to put this right. Here titles are dropped, everyone is referred to by his Christian name and a person's business and profession is kept well in the background. There is one big snag about it, however, you can't join until you retire! With these points in mind it is understandable that ministers would tend to form their own clubs and fellowships where they can meet as a Koinonia', sharing their joys and problems and perhaps have time for a little bit of gossip!

Rosemary Ministers' Fellowship

When I began my ministry in Dunlop Memorial I was soon aware of a need for fellowship where I could get guidance and encouragement. I had left a charge in the country where the church had a central place in the lives of my people, and where it was at the very heart of community life. In a new housing estate things were very different; while we had a nucleus of faithful members, for many the church was really irrelevant. For example I can recall more than one occasion when I visited a home, being received by the husband who politely told me that 'she' wasn't at home! For him the church might have something to offer women-folk but meant little in the man's world.

With this type of problem to deal with and many others I was delighted to receive an invitation to join a 'cell' – this was the 'in' word at that time. The idea came originally from Communism where a cell was a group of Communist members who were pledged to meet together and to work together to forward their cause. Not for the first time, Christians have taken a pagan idea and put it in a Christian setting. So the cell which I joined was made up of a group of Christian ministers which met once a fortnight from 9.30 am to 11.00 am for prayer, Bible study and a bit of chat. We didn't have many rules but there were a few disciplines that we tried to observe. One of these, the ensuring of one day off in the week was something that we aimed at but seldom achieved. The others applied mainly to our devotional life. We were expected to set aside at least half-an-hour each morning for prayer and Bible meditation and every Sunday morning to remember in prayer all other members of the group as in their church they proclaimed the Word and led their people in Worship.

The group at first met in Newington Presbyterian Church but later transferred to the new Rosemary Church on the North Circular Road and took on the name of Rosemary Ministers' Fellowship. The numbers varied from time to time but in those early days there were nine. Eric Borland (Rosemary), Ernest Brown (Seaview), Andrew Crooks (Bethany), Donald Gillies (Agnes Street), Norman Heaney (Newington), James Irvine (Alexandra), Ivor Lewis (Berry Street), James McFarland (Sinclair Seamen's) and myself (Dunlop Memorial).

To prevent our fellowship becoming too self-centred we decided that from time to time we would produce a series of sermons on a particular theme, in the hope that we might be invited to share these 'masterpieces' with a number of congregations. Each member was given a particular aspect of the theme and his task was to present an address on this, to be scrutinised by the other members of the group. Each in turn came along and read what he thought was an excellent effort, the result of much time and thought, but when he heard the comments of the others – the truth being spoken in love – he usually saw things differently! Sometimes it meant re-writing the address but in the end everyone felt that the exercise had been well worthwhile as we eventually possessed a sermon that had the imprimatur of the whole group.

The series which I best remember was based on the title 'My Faith', including such aspects as, 'My Faith and my Income', 'My Faith and my Work'. This series was produced in a number of churches including Ballywalter Presbyterian. I had reason to remember this service very clearly. It was arranged that the services would be held on a number of successive Sunday evenings. When my turn came along I had trouble with my voice at the morning service in Dunlop Memorial, but felt that it would be all right for the evening service in Ballywalter. Now this didn't happen and while I spent the afternoon resting my voice and trying out the usual home remedies, if anything, it became worse. By this time it was too late to find a replacement and so I had to set off hoping for the best.

I began the service in the pulpit but soon realised that I wasn't being heard (no P/A system in those days), so I came down to the reading desk apologising for my whispering and suggested that if they listened very carefully they might hear something. Well, I got through somehow and after the service a well-meaning elder said to me, 'You must come back sometime when we could hear you!'

There is so much that one could write about the R.M.F. and the colourful characters that composed it but space does not permit. May I just say this, that in days when some ministers appear to be under considerable strain, membership of a group like this could mean the difference between a breakdown and a happy, successful ministry.

Visit to Crieff

In the winter of 1959, the Belfast churches had a visit from the evangelist of the Church of Scotland. Rev D. P. Thompson. His sincerity and enthusiasm made a deep impression on all who heard him speak. He was at that time involved in a big project – the conversion of a parish church in Crieff, St Ninian's, to a training centre for members of his church. Someone got the idea that a group of us, mainly ministers in North Belfast, might consider visiting the new centre if this were possible. 'D.P.' as he was affectionately called, was delighted with the idea and right away began to make arrangements.

On 13th May 1959, ten ministers set sail for Scotland, having watched

Before the days of the drive-on method!

anxiously as our two cars were hoisted aboard the ferry. We had a pleasant run through the Burns country and then headed north for Crieff. When we arrived our host, 'D.P.' looked rather tired and untidy and soon we discovered the reason why. The task of converting the old church to a conference centre was far from complete and he had been working night and day to make our accommodation as comfortable as possible. He had done a wonderful job but the end product was certainly not 4 star standard! Another little shock was to discover that our outing would certainly not be a holiday. We gasped as we saw the programme that he had arranged for us, commencing at 7.00 am and going on until bed-time, with a couple of hours off in the afternoon. But if 'D.P.' set a high standard for others, he led by example – one could have heard him pounding away on his old typewriter at 3 o'clock in the morning! However, our spirits were not dampened by the prospects of a busy weekend. In almost every group of this type there is sure to be a joker, someone who is an endless source of fun and life. In our case we had two, Alfred Martin and James McFarland. To coin a phrase, there was never a dull moment but there

Our two 'jokers', Alfie Martin and Jim McFarland.

was one very sad one. On the Saturday afternoon word came through that Eric Borland's brother had died suddenly in Londonderry. This was a great shock to Eric and he decided to return home immediately. It presented quite a serious problem as one of our cars belonged to him and if he were to take his car with him some of us would have had difficulty in getting back to Stranraer. But very generously and showing great faith in my driving he left his car in my hands. There was just one condition – that I should drive him to Glasgow where he could board the ferry for Belfast. We missed Eric greatly as he had much to contribute to our discussion. We could only assure him of our prayers and deep sympathy in his sudden bereavement.

'D.P.' had chosen as his theme for the conference, 'The Church in To-morrow's World', and with the assistance of some outside speakers, brought a tremendous challenge to us all.

An invitation came from one of the local parish churches to provide a preacher for the Sunday morning service. We felt that this should go to our senior member. Alfred Martin. Fortunately he had brought a sermon with

Burns' Country – Brig O'Doon, associated with Tam O'Shanter.

him, probably one of his 'travellers' – a favourite sermon that goes the rounds! So armed with this and accompanied by his close friend James McFarland, Alfred set off for morning worship, the rest of us went to various services in the district, very happy to sit in the pew.

A little incident happened after Alfred's service which showed the delightful forthrightness of his friend James. Walking down the aisle after the service, he overheard two ladies discussing the sermon. One said, 'I do wish they wouldn't have these Irishmen in our pulpit for I just can't understand them.' That was too much from the man from Belfast's dockland. Like a flash he turned round and let her have it, 'Woman dear,' he said, 'what are you talking about, didn't you hear the Gospel this morning?' As far as I can recollect that was the end of the conversation!

We left Crieff on Monday morning after a very inspiring and helpful time and having expressed thanks to 'D.P.' for his tireless efforts to make the conference worthwhile, we set off for Edinburgh hoping to visit the General Assembly which opened that afternoon. We were in time to see the very dignified procession to the Assembly Hall and being ministers of a sister church, we were given special seats in the gallery.

It was a very solemn occasion and most inspiring but perhaps we missed the informality and occasional humour of our Assembly. We felt that here was a church that was facing up to its problems seriously; 'D.P' had spoken to us of the problem of falling membership and warned us that the same thing could happen here. Forty years later his words are coming true as most of the major denominations are facing a very similar situation.

As we headed for home we felt that one of the most beneficial effects of the whole venture was a really strong bond of friendship that had built up amongst us and which has continued down the years.

> *'They spent their time in learning from the apostles, taking part in the fellowship, and sharing in the fellowship meals and prayers.'*

Acts 2: 43, Good News Bible

24

Attaining Great Heights!

Brought up on a farm in the years of the Depression one became keenly aware of the need to live economically, indeed that was the only way to survive and those who didn't usually came to the wall.

Today the word mortgage, which is so essential to young people setting up home, still has for me a rather sinister ring about it, the reason being that in earlier times, farmers got a mortgage on their land, not to build a new house on it but usually to help 'make ends meet' and to pay off debts. Sometimes if they weren't able to pay the high interest rates involved, the money-lender closed in and eviction followed. A very sad day in my childhood was when this happened to a close neighbour and he and his family, children with whom I played, had to leave their home and head for the wilds of Saskatchewan in Canada.

Brought up in this environment one found it easy to accept the Biblical attitude towards material possessions – that we are but stewards of the gifts God has given us and that we must use wisely the resources around us. This concept must certainly become more real and more vital if we are to hand on to those who come after us a world that is not desperately impoverished.

And, of course, what applies to the use of the world's resources applies also to the running of a congregation, but here there is little opportunity to waste resources or be extravagant, for it usually requires all income to meet commitments. With this in mind I tended at times to resort to voluntary labour or DIY as we call it today. I did this for two reasons, firstly because it usually saved the congregation quite a lot financially and secondly and perhaps more importantly, it helped to create a spirit of fellowship and co-operation amongst members, coupled with lots of banter while the work proceeded. I was fortunate that in my various congregations there was always a group willing to have a go at the task in hand.

So in First Dromara when we were faced with the problem of damp penetration in the front wall of the church, we knew that putting it right would be a costly operation, but almost immediately it was pointed out that much of the work could be done on a voluntary basis. This was agreed and the first phase in the operation was to remove all plaster from the wall. This did not require any great skill, just a pair of strong hands and plenty of perseverance! Eventually the job was completed and the expert who came to treat the rising damp was very satisfied with our work. We then employed the best plasterer available and his work was top grade.

The next task was the painting of the wall and right away up popped the D.I.Y. boys who were quite sure that they could take this in their stride, especially as one of our members, Leslie Hamilton, was a professional painter and offered to supervise the work and to cope with any difficulties that might arise. The system worked well and the end-product was a wall that really enhanced the appearance of the building.

But there was a snag which reminds me of the old story told about the minister who, after twenty-five years of faithful service, received from his congregation a beautiful oil painting in appreciation of his work. Both he and his wife were delighted and chose for it a position in their sitting-room where it could be seen most advantageously. The picture looked really well but it was so colourful and fresh that it made the wallpaper look drab and faded. They decided to have the room completely re-decorated and that made a big change, but (you saw it coming!), they right-away realized that the carpet was quite badly worn and would have to be replaced. In the end the minister said that this picture was the most costly gift he had ever received!

Something similar happened in our church. Beside the new wall, the other walls looked really dull and the only answer was to include these in the scheme. The painters never hesitated – they just donned their dungarees again and armed with paint brushes got on with the job. Part of the team went up to the gallery and completed the wall painting there. It was then that they realised that the ceiling was in need of a coat of varnish – beside all the new painting it looked quite neglected! So some well-meaning lad decided to try a little varnish in the corner of the ceiling just to see how it would look; here the ceiling was within easy reach. The result of his effort was remarkable as the wood was really transformed, so our friend decided to extend the little patch and to varnish a further section. By this time he was joined by others and before long the ceiling area over the gallery had got a good coat of varnish.

This was all very commendable but for one thing: it left a large section in the centre of the ceiling untouched and untouchable from the gallery, it could

First Dromara: An interior view of this beautiful old Church.

only be reached from the ground floor using scaffolding. However, somehow it had to be done so we got together and one member came up with what seemed to be the answer. He thought he might be able to borrow a mobile scaffolding but it would be available for one day only, the following Thursday. A phone call confirmed that it would be possible. The scaffolding duly arrived on Wednesday evening and it was erected with a view to an early start next morning. A reasonable number of our members turned up around 9.00 am and it seemed that the work could be completed easily in one day, although I did notice that most members of the team were no longer teenagers! We made final preparations and then came the moment of truth – who was going to do the varnishing'? The men were all keen to help but one by one they had to withdraw – one had no head for heights, another couldn't climb up and a third couldn't work over his head. In the end it was left to a young apprentice from Ervine's mill and myself to tackle the job. Now I had been blessed with a good head for heights and always enjoyed a spot of painting, but to varnish a ceiling some twenty-five feet above floor level was somewhat different!

In fairness to the helpers, they tried to talk me out of it but to no avail! So, after some chat and banter the lad and I made the ascent and began the work, but my mate wasn't tall enough to reach the ceiling without considerable effort. The result was that he was putting more varnish over himself and over me than he was putting on the ceiling! So as tactfully as possible I told him that he might be better just to return to his job at the mill. This left me in the position of the prophet of old who called out in his hour of crisis, 'And I, even I only, am left.'

But I wasn't really alone for I had good support and encouragement on the floor and to see the ceiling take on a new appearance made it all worthwhile. In addition, as the scaffolding had to be moved quite frequently I was able to come down and have a rest whilst this was being done.

By 5.00 pm the job was finished and I also was about finished! When I came home for tea I didn't, of course, tell my wife what I had been doing. She thought I looked rather tired and my reply was that standing around all day was indeed tiring! This wasn't really dishonest for I didn't say at what height I had been standing! Months later someone spilled the beans and all she said was, 'There's no point in talking to that man of mine!' But she made me promise that I wouldn't do that kind of thing again and I have faithfully kept that promise!

25

It Can Happen

I am certainly not a mind-reader but sometimes while talking to people about Divine Healing, I may possibly have a fair idea of what is going on in their thinking. Perhaps they are comparing the ministry of Jesus while here upon earth with what goes on today in the Church's ministry of healing. They recall how when Jesus was confronted by suffering and disease, He simply touched the sick one or spoke a word of command and there invariably followed wonderful healing experiences. I can imagine the doubter saying 'Why don't you have results like this in modern times?'

There is no easy answer to such feelings and comments, but we would point out that Jesus operated on a dimension not available to us. He was divine as well as human while we who minister in His Name, are just human, weak and sinful. In spite of our unworthiness however, from time to time, remarkable things do happen. I recall one such experience.

Our Prayer Healing Group usually met for prayer about half-an-hour before the mid-week service. It consisted of a cross-section of our congregation, housewives, factory workers, business people etc. but all had one thing in common, a strong belief in the power of prayer to heal and to bring blessing.

Dick, a very enthusiastic member, worked in a mill in the east of the city and in his workplace certainly didn't 'hide his light under a bushel', but often talked to his mates about the work that was going on in our congregation. I am sure he got many a rebuff but nothing could daunt Dick. A brief account of his background might be of interest.

He was brought up in west Belfast in a pretty tough environment and early in life he got involved in the ways of the world, and that is putting it mildly, indeed to some he became known as 'the terror of the Shankill'. People carefully avoided him especially on Saturday nights when he had had more than enough to drink. Sometimes he would take a few of his cronies home for a drinking party, while his wife escaped upstairs and locked her door.

Then one night as he made his way home, he passed a corner where a man was preaching. He didn't stop nor did he hear a word that he said, but the picture of that preacher stuck in his mind. When he arrived home he could think of nothing else and eventually went upstairs, got down on his knees and asked the Lord for mercy and forgiveness. Almost immediately a great peace entered his heart and he became what St Paul would have described as 'a new man in Christ'. He later moved into our estate and was soon very active in the work of the church – one of our most dedicated members. He had a great sense of humour and I can recall him describing his earlier days when he said that the soles of his shoes were so thin that if he had stepped on a penny he could have told whether it was heads or tails!

Now back to the mill where he worked. Amongst the employees was a young woman who had been involved in an accident and as a result suffered severe headaches, indeed she was seldom free from pain. She had spent some time in hospital and everything possible had been done but the headaches persisted. Her condition had worsened and as a result of several falls she was in danger of losing her job.

Dick told her of our little group and invited her to come along some evening. The following week we met as usual for prayer remembering especially those in our congregation who were seriously ill. Towards the end of the prayer time there was a timid knock on the vestry door and someone entered the room. We continued and when our prayers were over I saw a stranger standing near the door I asked her if she had come for ministry or to seek prayers for a friend. She replied that she had come for ministry but that it was now unnecessary and then she related a truly remarkable experience.

She had gladly accepted the invitation to attend our group but when she got to the church, the pain in her head was so severe that she felt she couldn't sit through even a short meeting, so she stood outside the church for quite a long time while she struggled to cope with her pain and her fears. Eventually, realising that she might miss an opportunity of blessing she made a great effort, pulled herself together and headed for the vestry.

What followed is hard to believe but I relate it exactly as she told it to us. It seemed that as she entered the room, she felt possessed by a strange power, warm and comforting and as a result her whole body began to tingle and one thing soon became apparent – the violent pain in her head began to ease until it completely disappeared. Hence her reply that she didn't need to come for ministry!

Jesus, speaking to the man at the Pool of Bethesda, asked him if he wished to be made whole. The word 'whole' surely meant much more than physical healing. Certainly in the vestry that night the healing process was not confined to the removal of a severe headache, it also permeated the realm of the spirit; that young woman had been a very nominal Christian but suddenly it all became clear and personal, she knew 'whom she believed'. She returned some weeks later and spoke at our mid-week service, describing her experience and its effect on her life. She had become actively involved in Christian work which included the forming of a Bible Study Group in the mill.

There can be only one explanation for all this, a break-through into the here and now of the power of the eternal Christ, and having witnessed it once we become assured that it can happen again and again. There was a glorious manifestation of that power on the Shankill Road on that fateful Saturday night when Dick was set free from the chains that held him, and again in the vestry when a young woman was freed from pain and anxiety.

In the post-Resurrection days the disciples were thrilled as Jesus kept appearing to them until they believed that He might reveal His presence and power at any moment. That belief plays an important part in the ministry of Divine Healing; in other words, the compassionate Christ is the same yesterday, today and always.

26

They Come in Threes

The summer of 1988 had been a very disappointing one, showers and bright intervals but no real heat. Then about the middle of August, the weathermen began to talk of high pressure coming in from the continent and soon the country was bathed in lovely sunshine. We were keen to make the most of it and having been offered the use of the Corkey caravan for a week at Castlerock, we were soon on our way. The caravan was free, a gift from the family, and we would just be having our normal food so we didn't expect to be spending very much on this holiday or so we thought!

There was just one little job we had to do for Heather and Colin – not much in return for the use of their caravan. For some time they had been thinking about changing their estate car – they liked to have a biggish car as they had a biggish dog which, like Mary's little lamb, was sure to go wherever they went! They felt that a new model would cost too much and were looking for a good second-hand one. They had spotted such in the 'Tele', located in the Coleraine Garage. They asked us to have a look at it and to report back to them. This we were glad to do but the car in question had done a big mileage and looked the worse for wear, so we felt it would not be suitable.

However, they decided to come to Coleraine and to have a look around for themselves. They agreed that the car which we had looked at was not for them, but by this time the salesman had joined us and like all good salesmen was keen to be helpful! He hadn't any other estate cars but suggested that they would really be better to buy a new one. At first they turned the idea down completely but after a little gentle persuasion from the salesman and the offer of a very good price for their old car in part-exchange, they finally capitulated and the deal was completed!

Now up to this point, Queenie and I had been simply spectators of all that was going on. At this stage the salesman turned his attention on us, perhaps beginning to think that the McComb family were a soft touch!

We had no intention of changing our car, Peugeot 205, which we had purchased second-hand some two years previously at a cost of three thousand,

Old for new – awaiting the part-exchange!

six hundred pounds. It was going very well with no sign of rust – very important in those days. The salesman, however, had other ideas and had a look round the car, with an eye for bumps and rust spots. He seemed quite pleased with what he saw so he resorted to his 'wee book'. After another look at the car he came back with an offer, part-exchange for a new car, three thousand, six hundred pounds, the exact amount I had paid for it two years previously! I could scarcely believe my ears but tried to conceal my surprise. 'Thank you very much,' I said, as calmly as possible, 'but, of course, we'll have to give the matter a lot of thought and perhaps let you know tomorrow.' It didn't really take long to decide the matter and next day we returned to order a new car and, of course, a Peugeot!

Now our younger daughter, Carol, and her husband, Samuel, had been kept informed of all these buyings and sellings and feeling that they were missing something, decided to join us in Coleraine!

Probably of the three families, they were most in need of a new car for their old '205' had done a lot of heavy work and was certainly showing signs of wear. Their difficulty, however, was that just then they had been involved in considerable outlay and did not feel like facing the extra burden of a new car.

By this time the salesman was really on his toes and his approach was to express sympathy to them, being left out of the spending spree! But he had a car that had just arrived and he would like them to have a look at it anyway. It was a special model with all kinds of extras and, of course, they fell for it! There was just one little obstacle: the matter of cost, and they knew that their old car wouldn't figure too highly in the salesman's 'wee book'. But they, like the rest of us, got a pleasant surprise and in a matter of minutes the whole thing was settled and the salesman had got his hat-trick!

Now arose the question of delivery. The cars, unfortunately, were available at different times so we decided to make a day of it and to accept delivery of all three cars on the same day. So on Saturday 20th August we set off for Coleraine driving our three old Peugeots. It rained most of the way but when we got to the garage the sun was shining.

The Manager, Mr Tannahill, had really gone to town in his preparations for this special occasion. Photographs were to be taken, the three ladies each received a lovely bouquet of flowers and all were entertained to coffee. Then in our brand new Peugeots we drove to the caravan at Castlerock for a celebratory lunch, after which we proudly set off for home.

It was a day that we shall always remember and while the three cars have all been replaced, we are all still driving Peugeots! If this story ever became known to the people at Peugeot headquarters, I'm sure that it would result in more flowers!

27

Women have the Last Word

The title for this little snippet was certainly borne out in an experience that happened to my friend and neighbour, Rev Grant Smith. He was the kind of person about whom endless stories are told, some true and most somewhat exaggerated! For example, when his name would be mentioned in company I have often heard some one say 'Oh that's the wee man who sleeps in the bath!' Well that is a kind of half-truth – he didn't sleep in the bath but in the bathroom and he had good reason for doing so. He suffered from a mild form of asthma and when at bedtime he moved from a warm living-room to a cold bedroom upstairs, he began to cough and this went on for quite a long time. Then he made an important discovery, that the bathroom with its hot-press was warmer than his bedroom, so he promptly moved his bed to it and found that his coughing was greatly reduced! We are all familiar with the phrase 'poetic licence', perhaps there is also a 'story-telling licence' permitting the narrator to add a few little titbits as in this case – Grant sleeping not just in the bathroom but in the bath!

I can however vouch for the accuracy of the following story as I heard it from Grant's own lips, just a few days after it all happened, and although he was small in stature he was big enough to enjoy a joke against himself.

At this time there was founded in our Church an organisation under the title, 'The Women's Home Mission', which was meant to do at home something of the work done overseas by 'The Women's Foreign Mission'. The first president was Mrs A W Neill, wife of the minister of First Armagh. She was the kind of person who couldn't do things by halves. She put her boundless enthusiasm into this office and her vision for this new organisation was to have a branch in every congregation.

One day she met Grant Smith when he was doing a little shopping in town. After a few remarks about the weather and their health she gave him a bird's-eye view of the new organisation, suggesting that it could he very helpful in his charge. Grant was quite impressed, with the result that Mrs Neill offered to go out some evening to speak to the ladies about it. But there was a difficulty

– it would be very hard to get the women to attend a week-night meeting as many of them would have to walk along dark and lonely lanes. But Mrs Neill was not to be put off by this; she would be happy to come to the Sunday service and to speak to the women in church. Grant, always keen to help his people, agreed to this and a Sunday was fixed for the visit.

Sometime later that afternoon he met a friend and told him about the arrangement with Mrs Neill. Now this man, noted for his leg-pulling ability responded, 'Surely you're not going to have a woman in your pulpit.' Grant, unfortunately, took this approach seriously and being a person who tended to act impulsively, next day sent Mrs Neill a telegram with this message. 'Regret our arrangement has to be cancelled – 1 Cor, 14 v 34: Let your women keep silent in the churches. Grant.'

I never heard what Mrs Neill's reaction was, but she must have been disappointed, although knowing Grant, she may just have smiled, and soon forgot about it. But he was not allowed to do that. Soon the weekend arrived when Mrs Neill would have been due to visit Grant's congregation of Armaghbrague. On the Saturday afternoon snow began to fall, just fine flakes but speeded along by a gale-force wind. At bedtime people looking out realised that they were in for a real blockade as wreaths of snow were forming up to ten feet high. By Sunday afternoon the roads around Armaghbrague were impassible as far as cars were concerned and only a few brave souls ventured out on foot. Now Grant had never owned or driven a car, he was completely dependent on a faithful taxi driver from Keady who never seemed to let him down. But this was different. There was no hope of getting Grant transported three miles to his church up in the hills, which meant that no minister turned up for the service and not many worshippers either, about twenty in all.

The elders present were naturally upset as no one felt capable of entering the pulpit, but help was at hand in the form of two Faith Mission Pilgrims who were conducting a mission in the area. When approached they gladly agreed and both of them entered the pulpit, conducting a very acceptable service.

So Grant, refusing to have a woman in his pulpit, finished up having two presiding there! I can imagine our womenfolk of today having a chuckle as they read this little cameo of church life in the old days. How attitudes have changed in the past fifty years – today we have women elders doing excellent work in our Kirk Sessions, and a strong team of women ministers who have shown us that, as in medicine, law and other professions, women have gifts to offer and qualities of leadership that even the critics have got to admire.

I'm sure there must be a moral in this little episode but suffice to say that in spite of the great superiority (imagined?) of men, we just couldn't do without the ladies!

28

Gardens

Most of us, as we walk around a lovely garden, have quoted the well known lines from the poem 'God's Garden':

> *The kiss of the sun for pardon*
> *The song of the birds for mirth*
> *One is nearer God's heart in a garden*
> *Than anywhere else on earth.*

Lovely words these may be but they are true only in certain circumstances. Imagine yourself, for example, on a lovely summer evening relaxing in a deck chair which rests on a well manicured lawn, surrounded by rose beds in full bloom with the perfume of sweet peas wafted towards you by a gentle breeze, and you could possibly be aware of a heavenly presence. However, I feel that at times there may be more truth in my rather unkind parody:

> *The heat of the sun is killing*
> *The spade is breaking my back.*
> *You can be nearer despair in a garden*
> *Than in jungle without a track!*

I have experienced both these conditions in my attempts at gardening.

To begin with, my father was very fond of a garden but as a farmer he just hadn't time for it. I remember him telling us about a cousin who came down from the city to visit her country relations. She had a stroll around the homestead and then in a censorious voice said to my father, 'Tom, have you not got a garden?' 'Oh, yes,' was his reply, 'I've got a large garden and I would like you to see it.' And then he took her to a field of about six acres in which was growing a crop of Skerry potatoes and they were in full bloom, a truly lovely sight. 'That,' he said to his cousin, 'is my garden.' I'm sure she got the message! In later life, however, gardening became his hobby and possibly something of his enthusiasm rubbed off on me.

My first garden was attached to the manse at Redrock and my predecessor, in spite of poor health, had left it in pretty good shape, although there was much clearing up work to be done – pruning apple trees, clipping hedges, weeding, etc. For me this garden had a special attraction, four very good plum trees. I've always had a weakness for Victoria plums, and the fruit of these trees, while somewhat smaller, had the same delicious flavour. With minimum attention they produced the same bumper crop year after year.

A little point worth mentioning here is the fact that while the plums and apples were easily seen from the nearby road, I don't think that any of the local lads ever attempted to help themselves. We had a very different experience elsewhere. One summer I was offered a manse near the north coast for the month of August in return for being responsible for the conduct of Sunday services. This coast has much to offer the visitor, wonderful scenery, excellent golf courses and an air that is really invigorating, so we looked forward with great anticipation to our holiday.

When we arrived the minister gave me some guidance as to my duties which were not too onerous. He referred to a very good apple tree in the garden and unlike the unfortunate couple in the Garden of Eden, we were told we could eat the apples and then he added the words, 'That is if you can get them.'

I asked him for an explanation and he told me that invariably just before the apples were fully ripe, they disappeared! I made up my mind that this would not happen while we were around. The month passed quickly in spite of very unsettled weather, and then in the last week we had a glorious day and decided to spend the afternoon on the local beach and to have a picnic tea there. We returned about 7.00 pm after a wonderful time on the beach and as we drove past the apple tree – yes, you've guessed it, there wasn't an apple on it!

Our next garden was in North Belfast and was quite small, requiring little attention. This was fortunate as the task of building a new church in the nearby estate took up most of my time. What lay ahead as we moved to the new city of Craigavon was a very different setting – just a mass of clay with a very light layer of top-soil covering it! I was tempted to leave it alone but I've always felt that a house without a garden of some kind is certainly not a home. A further point was that one day the estate manager called to welcome us, and told us that we were really living in the 'Malone Road' area of the new city. I wondered what it must be like in the 'Sandy Row' area!

The remarkable thing was that in spite of really adverse conditions some things grew very well – we had lovely potatoes and peas that had an excellent flavour; flowers, however, weren't so successful.

But perhaps the greatest challenge was to come when we moved to the First Dromara Manse. The extensive grounds had been neglected for many years, my two predecessors not being keen gardeners! But the great asset was that once the ground had been cleared we could start from scratch with our planning.

Perhaps I should have employed an expert to guide us but I knew that this could finish up in a considerable outlay and already a lot had been spent on the manse, so it was a case of D.I.Y. The first job was to get the drive into order and this meant re-surfacing and kerbing. Here the menfolk of the Church were most helpful and undertook to be responsible for the kerbing under the guidance of a young member, Desmond Elliott, a qualified civil engineer, so our little job didn't present any problems to him. One lovely evening as the work was drawing to a close, my wife had brought out supper and we were sitting around chatting when we heard strange noises coming from the eaves of the roof. Looking up we saw an endless stream of bats emerge – someone began to count and estimated that there must have been over a hundred in the flock or whatever a flight of bats is called!

Now this explained something. Our girls had their bedroom at the front of the house and they complained about hearing 'squeally' sounds overhead at night. We didn't take this too seriously as children can easily exaggerate things but now we knew it was not imagination but a big colony of bats. And the amazing thing is that as far as we knew the bats never returned – that night for some reason they sought fresh pastures. Our younger daughter put forward the explanation that the bats had heard bad reports about the McCombs!

One further point of interest in the planning programme was the siting of the fruit garden. I chose what I thought was a suitable site, near the rear of the house and getting plenty of sunlight, but did not realise that about one foot below the surface there was solid rock. I think I would have given up but for the help and encouragement of an older member, Willie McLaughlin. He had worked in a quarry in his younger days and knew the right way to split a rock. But apart from his work I greatly appreciated his 'crack'. Rock-splitting was tiring and from time to time we had to stop for a rest. Willie would have a wee smoke and regale me with stories about First Dromara in the past. He had been around the manse doing various jobs down the years and had known the ministers very well especially their little peculiarities, for example, Sidney Jamison, who was noted for his skill as a wrestler and was prepared to take on any young man in the congregation in a wrestling match!

An additional pleasure for me was the fact that from our site we had a perfect view of the sunset, and having lived for thirteen years under the shadow of the Cavehill, where one never saw the sun setting, that was joy indeed. My interest in sunsets goes back a long time. My mother had a friend who was something of a mystic and who spent a few weeks at our home every summer. I can recall a moment when my sisters brought her a bunch of primroses; she seemed to see some almost divine beauty in them but to us they were just primroses. And it sometimes happened when a few of us were playing football in the field beside our home that she would stand at the gate watching, not the potential 'stars' displaying their skills with a football, but the sun going down behind the Derry mountains! Of course, we were sure that she was 'crackers' but with the passing of the years I must admit that I have come to share in her appreciation of the sunset. To stand on a summer evening at that gate into the field at home (the footballers would not be there, but there would still be the beauty and glory of the setting sun) I would be very happy indeed. Perhaps I also have become 'crackers'!

But back to the rock-breaking. With Willie's patience and encouragement, the garden began to take shape. Although as I sometimes said, apart from the basic fruit and vegetables, I hadn't time to garden. All I could do was to try to told back the jungle by weeding, grass-cutting, hedge-clipping etc! However, when it was in order it looked really well and added much to the appearance of the old but beautiful manse.

And then last scene of all, as Shakespeare would have said, my retirement garden in Newcastle. As the house had been let for several years, the garden suffered from neglect; indeed it was just like a piece of the hillside with an occasional whin bush peeping through and lots of well established weeds. However, it was small and I now had plenty of time to spend on it and to do something which I had planned for a long time – to grow some really good roses. In this matter I got a lot of help and encouragement from the local Gardening Society, many of whose members are excellent gardeners.

I had the privilege for several years of visiting the senior members of our

Retirement garden in Newcastle.

congregation and I would say that one of the greatest joys of gardening is to take a bunch of lovely roses to someone who is old or ill or lonely. The look of pleasure on their face says it all; I don't think that any other flowers would have this effect.

In the picture of the Holy Jerusalem that we have in the Book of Revelation, Chapter xxi, we note that the street is made of pure gold. Quite honestly that would not attract me very much, but if the street were lined with lovely roses, especially red roses, that would add much to the heavenly delights.

While there are many things in our province that tend to depress us, there are also things that cheer and encourage us. One of these is the fact that many of the fine houses being built throughout our land have well planned gardens around them. Dare I suggest that this could make a contribution to peace in our province greater than much of the talking that goes on? If every home had even a small patch of garden where a few flowers could be grown and children taught to tend and value them, it just might help to reduce violence, remove hatred and build a happier and more beautiful province.

29

Healing – Absent and Instant

We are all familiar with that remarkable scene in Capernaum when the centurion came to Jesus seeking healing for his servant who suffered from palsy. This centurion was a very modest man – he felt he wasn't good enough to receive Christ into his home; he was also a man of great faith, he believed that there was no need for the Lord to come at all; He just had to say the word and his servant would be healed. Jesus marvelled at his faith and immediately acceded to his request and at that moment the servant was healed, a wonderful example of absent and instant healing.

Now there may be people who can do that kind of thing today but I haven't met them. Someone may say 'What about the person who possesses a charm?' Yes, I have heard remarkable claims being made in this field and I had the opportunity of investigating one such case. An elderly man was suffering from a severe nose-bleed and it was decided to send, not for the doctor, but for a person who had a charm for this trouble. His son was sent off on his bicycle to get in touch with him. It meant travelling quite a distance and unfortunately the man was not at home and this meant a considerable wait. Eventually he returned, listened to the request and simply said, 'Away home and the bleeding will have stopped when you get there.' And that's how it was; of course it wasn't long until it was being told that the bleeding stopped at the exact moment that the man with the charm spoke the word.

I heard this story and decided to make a few enquiries. I discovered a certain vagueness as to the time when the bleeding stopped and also that it hadn't stopped suddenly but quite gradually. In addition all the usual home-made remedies were being applied throughout. So really the bleeding had taken a normal course, severe for a time and then gradually easing off. I certainly could not regard it as a case of distant healing, but in adopting this attitude I am not discounting all the 'charm cures' which I have heard of from people whom I regard as sensible and dependable – quite honestly I don't understand how such things happen.

However, in the sphere of prayer I am on more solid ground and could

The Chapel in Church House, Belfast, presented by the Very Rev A.J. Weir, in memory of his parents, Rev Andrew and Mrs Weir. A Service of Intercessory Prayer and Ministry to the Sick is held here every Thursday morning.

quote a number of cases where as a result of prayer, distance was not an obstacle, and instant healing followed. Two in particular come to mind. The first concerned a lady who was seriously ill following major surgery. Normally in such cases each day brings a little improvement until the patient is fully restored. In this case it was not so for if anything she was losing ground. Every few minutes a check was made on her condition but there were no signs of improvement. Then around 11.30 am on this particular day the whole situation changed dramatically, to the amazement of the staff, and from that time her improvement was steady, until she returned to normal well-being.

Now all this happened on a Thursday morning and at that time the weekly meeting of intercessory prayer and ministry was taking place in the chapel of Church House. A close friend of the sick lady had come seeking prayer for her. The group of intercessors were deeply moved by the seriousness of the situation and fervent prayers were offered on her behalf. It was around this time that the remarkable change in her condition was noted by the hospital staff.

Some weeks later I happened to be conducting the weekly service in the chapel and I referred to this wonderful answer to prayer but pointed out that we must not claim too much as it was possible that the crisis, the moment of change in the illness just coincided with the time of prayer. At that point a lady stood up and said, 'May I speak?' I was somewhat surprised for seldom is a minister interrupted in his address but I replied, 'Of course, go ahead.'

Now this was the lady who had the remarkable hospital experience and who, unknown to me, had come to the service to give thanks. Right away she said it was not a coincidence but a definite answer to prayer. She went on to explain that as she got stronger she was shown some of the records of her illness while she was unconscious and lay between life and death, and the thing that really impressed her as she examined these reports, was the amazing change that took place around 11.30 am, baffling all concerned. She expressed sincere appreciation of the hospital staff who had sustained her during those trying hours; almost in tears she gave thanks to those who had prayed so earnestly for her, and to the Lord who had kept His promise, 'When thou passeth through the waters I will be with thee.'

I would like to refer to another case of absent healing which was equally impressive. This happened during a service in Sinclair Seamen's Church, Belfast. Early in each service we had a time of intercessory prayer for those who were too ill or too far away to attend personally. A woman came along very concerned about her neighbour who was crippled with rheumatoid arthritis. She was a prisoner in her little house, barely able to walk more than a few yards, although still in her fifties. She had been a keen knitter using her skill to help especially those in need. Now it seemed that this was all a thing of the past and she felt that her days of usefulness were over, but something very wonderful was soon to happen transforming her whole life.

There were at least two hundred people at the service, many of them what we called 'prayer partners', people who had come solely to join with us in praying for the sick. We remembered a number of people in our prayers including this lady committing each one into the hands of a loving Saviour.

Sometimes we wondered if our prayers really achieved very much as the feed-back was usually minimal. Not so in this case for a few days after the service I received a phone call from the neighbour who had put her name forward. She told me of an amazing change that had happened to her friend – all pain had gone and she was now able to go to the shop and carry her goods back. Well, my father's name was Thomas and that might fittingly have been handed on to me, for when I hear a story like that I tend to take it with a grain of salt! Those reports can easily be exaggerated and I like definite proof.

I decided to visit the lady and to find out for myself just what had happened. She lived in a small house in a street off the Crumlin Road in Belfast and when I arrived and told her who I was she invited me to come in and led me to her living room in quite a sprightly manner. The first thing I noticed was her knitting on a table beside her chair – she had begun to knit after a break of some three years. She was free from pain and able to do all her housework and then she told me something that really astounded me. She said that she intended coming to the next service of Divine Healing and she hoped to walk to it – a distance of over a mile! When I recovered from the shock, I asked for a favour – ministers have that awful habit of pushing people into jobs! I asked her if she would consider telling us at the service something of her experience. This came as a great surprise to her as she had never spoken in public, but she felt that she owed so much to the Healing Christ, she should attempt it. I suggested that she might write down a few lines and just read them to the congregation and this she agreed to consider.

What a thrill it was a month later to welcome her to our service after her walk from the Crumlin Road. She was naturally nervous as she rose to read the story of her healing to the large congregation. One could have heard a pin dropping and when she had finished this hush continued for a little while. It could be described only as heavenly peace and no one seemed to want to bring it to an end. We could indeed have said with Jacob, 'This is none other than the house of God and this is the gate of Heaven.'

Healing, absent or instant? Yes, it still can happen.

30

A Time to Smile

In the Book of Proverbs the writer makes a statement which has a very real bearing upon the ministry of healing, he says, 'A merry heart doeth good like a medicine.' This is wonderful news and advice both for the sick and those who minister to them. When we are suffering pain or under the cloud of a terminal disease, fun and joy can easily disappear from our lives, and yet some people manage to smile even in the darkest circumstances. Certainly while one experiences many heart-breaking occasions in this ministry, there are also times when the sun breaks through and smiles are the order of the day.

I think of a wonderful lady who has suffered much and is greatly handicapped but who hasn't forgotten how to smile and how to share that smile with others. Lily – she allowed me to use her name for she never thought that anyone would mention her in a book – came for ministry some ten years ago. Her sight had failed badly and because of a serious heart complaint, it was felt that surgery would be inadvisable. We had a little chat about the healing ministry of Jesus and then a time of prayer. Immediately afterwards she opened her handbag and looked intently at something. I asked her what she was doing and she replied, 'I've got my Bible here and I'm just testing my sight to see if there is any improvement.' Well, I think she was a little disappointed as there was no change, but a definite improvement came about a week later and has continued. As a result she has been able to knit hundreds of woollen squares for 'Save the Children Fund' and although she was approaching ninety years of age she undertook to knit ten knee rugs for the 'old ladies' in a local residential home! But she felt she must show her appreciation to me in some way so she wrote saying that she understood that I didn't accept a fee for my ministry, and instead she had put ten pounds in her mission box and had asked the Lord to put it to my credit! I can see the twinkle in her eye as she wrote those words!

Of course, there can be occasions when, if there is a smile, it is a very wry one. I think of one such moment. I had been invited to visit a man who was near the point of death. I never refuse such an invitation because while physical healing seldom occurs in these cases, yet there can be healing at a deep spiritual level. Here, as soon as I entered the home I was aware of a spirit of apathy, approaching opposition to my presence – I happen to be very sensitive to atmosphere which is not always a good thing! His wife took me to her husband's bedroom and, after a word of introduction, disappeared. He was in a semi-conscious state and I simply quoted a few familiar verses from Scripture and then in prayer committed him into the hands of a loving Saviour. But while this was happening, I was aware of quite a lot of noise and commotion downstairs which I thought was rather strange under the circumstances. When I came down, however, I was quickly ushered to the door, but one didn't have to be very observant to realise what was going on – rooms were being seated in preparation for the funeral! If there happened to be a smile on my face as I came away, it was certainly a sad one.

But back to a happier situation. One morning a lady came for ministry, suffering from deep depression. We had quite a long session, lasting almost two hours and without attempting to play the part of an amateur psychiatrist. I tried to bring her something of the healing peace of the Risen Christ. She seemed to have got some help and on leaving, perhaps realising that she had taken up a lot of my time, she said, 'Now one day I'll maybe be able to do something for you.' About a month after her visit I received a phone call from her. She seemed to be much brighter and was very pleased to tell me something. 'I've got the earplugs for you,' she said. I was puzzled and asked what they were for. 'Well,' she said, 'during our conversation I told you that often I woke up very early and being unable to go asleep again I would switch on the radio. This in turn would wake up my husband who never seemed to enjoy the radio at this early hour. Now,' she continued, 'at that stage you smiled for you said that the same thing sometimes happened in your home!' And then she went on to tell me that she thought of a special earplug which she felt might be helpful in this situation. They were obtainable only in London but she had managed to get some which she would forward right away. They duly arrived but the thought of Grandpa putting in earplugs at bedtime and going into a world of silence brought so much merriment to our family, especially our grandchildren, that I'm afraid I never used them! However, I greatly appreciated the kind thought that lay behind this gift and we still get a smile when we refer to the dear lady's attempt to solve our little problem!

I return to the proverb that speaks of the 'merry heart'. One evening after a service of healing, I spoke to a woman who had come forward to receive ministry. She looked very downcast, almost glum, and I asked her if she had been helped in any way by the service. 'Oh yes,' she replied, 'I got a lot of help.' And then I'm afraid I was a little naughty for my next words to her were, 'Forgive me saying this but you don't look as if you had received a blessing – you look sad and disappointed. Let's have a smile.' She was somewhat taken aback by my approach but soon the message got through and she actually gave a little chuckle as she said, 'I know what you mean.' In that moment of brightness she possibly got a second blessing!

Now it's easy to write about the blessing of the 'merry heart', the cheerful disposition, but someone enduring continual pain or suffering from a terminal disease may well call out in despair, 'But how does one achieve this quality of life?' Perhaps the best reply is to quote examples of people who have achieved just this. I mention two, one from the Early Church and the other from our everyday world.

We are all familiar with the Biblical one, Stephen, who was the first to die for the Christian Faith. We recall that as the stones rained down upon his defenceless head, he looked up to heaven, to his Lord and was given grace sufficient for his great need. The result, his face shone as the face of an angel. Now Stephen could never have done this on his own. It was indeed superhuman reaction, the result of the channel of love and power that existed between him and his Lord. But the questioner may point out that Stephen was a saint of Bible times and suggest that such things don't happen today: well, they do.

I recall being invited to a home where the mother, in her fifties, was confined to a wheelchair due to severe arthritis. I was told that she had been a great worker, always on the go, a source of help and joy to all around her. I expected to see someone depressed and frustrated, but that was certainly not the case; she was sitting in her wheelchair, serene and happy, and greeted me with a lovely smile. I thought this might just be a façade but as we talked together it became obvious that her spirit of happiness was deep within her. And then I noticed something on the wall opposite to where she sat, a little card which had been framed and which bore the words, 'Never lose sight of Jesus'. And that explained it all – during those weary years of suffering and disappointment, she had drawn on the wonderful resources that He makes available and had become 'more than conqueror'.

George Matheson may not have been thinking about a 'merry heart' when he wrote his famous hymn but the situation is very similar:

> *'My heart is weak and poor*
> *Until it master find;*
> *It has no spring of action sure –*
> *It varies with the wind.*
> *It cannot freely move,*
> *Till Thou has wrought its chain;*
> *Enslave it with Thy matchless love*
> *And deathless it shall reign.'*

31

To Pray without Ceasing

It is hard to know what exactly Paul meant by these words. They certainly can't be taken literally, meaning that every minute of every hour be taken up in prayer. The bus driver or the computer worker, while they may offer a little prayer for help when things go badly wrong, know full well that the task in hand demands their full attention at all times and this is true of many occupations.

But Paul was a pragmatist with his feet firmly planted on the ground. I suggest that this prayer exhortation means one or both of two things: firstly, that we should pray on every possible occasion, not only when the clouds gather but also when the sun shines; and secondly, being assured that a certain matter, such as a disease or a social evil, is not in God's Will, that we should persevere in our praying that what is wrong might be put right.

I would like to quote an example representing the latter point of view. In the summer of 1980, Jim, a middle-aged man, came to my home for ministry. One didn't have to ask what his trouble was for there were obvious signs of eczema on his hands and head. He had never known a day when he was completely free of this unpleasant skin disease. What struck me about him especially was the fact that in spite of having tried all possible sources of cure, he still had hope that one day he would be healed. This may have been due to the fact that both he and his wife were strong believers in the power of prayer. Often we hear people say that while there is life there is hope but it is also true to say that while there is hope there is also the possibility of life, especially if that hope is based on the healing love of the Saviour. While we all have to die sometime, only the good Lord knows exactly when, and to take from someone the hope of recovery often seems to hasten the end or worsen the condition. So Jim, in spite of past disappointments, had the hope that through the power of the living Christ he could be set free from his affliction.

The experience of ministering to him was really delightful for from the beginning there was a definite improvement in his condition, and after a number of lengthy counselling and prayer sessions he was completely healed. When the lame man at the Temple gate was healed through the ministry of Peter and John, we are told that he entered the Temple, walking and leaping and praising God. Jim, perhaps less exuberant, was also joyous in his praise to God for all that He had done for him.

At that time I happened to be editor of a magazine called *Christian Healing* and it occurred to me that an account of Jim's healing might be of interest to its readers. I asked Jim if he would kindly write me a brief report of his experience. To my surprise he hesitated and then he said, 'I may as well tell you that I can't write because as a child, owing to my disease, I was unable to go to school.' I regretted causing this embarrassment but his wife quickly solved the problem by saying that she would write it. I have retained that report and quote from it mainly the part describing his condition and experience in earlier life.

Jim's eczema began when he was three months old. His parents saw to it that he got all the medical attention available and when this failed tried nature cures and charms but the eczema persisted. He was able to go to school only for a day now and again and his arms were so badly affected that they had to be covered even when he went out to play with his friends. When we got married the disease seemed under control but in about two years' time it came back as bad as ever. It was nearly impossible for him to keep a job as he had to have hospital treatment two or three times each year and this meant several weeks at a time. As well as that he never slept until nearly morning and then if going to work, he had to spend almost an hour putting ointment all over his body. At times his skin was very dry and flaky and at other times it was weeping and bed-clothes had to be changed every day.

The doctors in the hospital were very good and tried various drugs and diets but nothing seemed to bring lasting relief. At home there were times when his underclothes had to be changed three times each day. Family life suffered when our family were young for we were never able to go for a holiday, indeed at times a family outing for a few hours wasn't possible.

Sometimes I became bitter, blaming God for our troubles but never losing faith and always I kept praying that Jim would be cured. Now our prayers have been answered and as a result of it all, our faith has become stronger. I know now what Job meant when he said that it didn't matter what would happen to him, he would still believe in his God.

That was seventeen years ago and I'm afraid I had lost touch with Jim and often wondered how he was keeping. The position was clarified recently when, out of the blue, I had a phone call from him, apologising for not contacting me much sooner and hoping to visit me in the near future, just to let me see how well he is! Apparently during those seventeen years he has been entirely free from any kind of skin disease and has been in constant employment.

Both he and his wife had prayed continually for healing. Now they continue to pray but the emphasis is on praise and gratitude to God for all that He has done for them. If through some form of modern technology it were possible to contact St Paul, I could tell him with some confidence that here were two people who took his exhortation seriously and who had 'prayed without ceasing'.

32

Mementoes

Most of us have in our possession articles which may not be very valuable but for us they have a special significance which makes them worth much more than their selling-price in the open market. An obvious example is a wedding ring – just a plain gold ring which if put up for sale might fetch only a few pounds but the happily married wife would not part with it for a hundred times that amount.

I happen to have at least two such objects – the first is a small rolling pin used for making pastry and made of bog oak which was given to me by a senior member of my first congregation. She was then approaching ninety years of age and loved to talk about the 'old days' and this I found fascinating. As a child there was no worry in her home about the diseases that today are associated with beef etc., for the only meat that ever appeared on their table was what she called 'American bacon', salted bacon imported from America. This delicacy was available only on the Sabbath. The staple diet was potatoes and lots of home-made bread and buttermilk. Of course they also had porridge, not the instant type that comes from a packet but from the whole meal that had to be steeped overnight before use.

This simple diet may have accounted for her good health – for example, on the occasion of her ninetieth birthday I called to see her and found her feeding her hens – she had, of course, forgotten all about this special birthday. Later looking back over the years she told me that she hadn't been to see her doctor over the previous fifty years! After a little chat about her hens when she pointed out the good layers and the ones that were always clockin', we went inside. I soon got her talking about her young days and from time to time she added interest to her memories by producing relevant articles from her little corner cupboard. Amongst these was a delightful little rolling pin which had been used by her grandmother in the local manor house.

Without thinking I admired this unusual article, so beautifully shaped that it was more a work of art than a kitchen utensil. Right away she said, 'I would like you to have this so just take it home with you.' Trying not to hurt her as I refused her kind offer, I explained to her that as the rolling pin had been so long in her family it must mean much to her and I felt she should keep it. 'Well', she replied, 'I'll keep it but before I pass on, I'll make sure you get it.'

As it happened I was the one that passed on, not to the Great Beyond but to the establishing of a new church in a north Belfast housing estate. Some three years later, a visitor who happened to be a neighbour of my old friend called at our home. He carried a small box and inside it the rolling pin! He explained that he had gone to visit her shortly before her death and as he was leaving her parting words were 'Make sure that Mr McComb gets the wee rolling pin'. And that is how it came into my possession. As I thought of the scene, an old lady in her nineties, at the end of life's journey and remembering a promise made years before, the tears weren't far from my eyes – what a glorious glimpse of real character.

The other memento also came from on old friend, Rev Joseph McKee, my predecessor in Redrock and Druminnis. When he moved from the manse he found it necessary to have an auction to help solve the old problem of putting a quart into a pint container – the contents of a large manse into a small house. On the night before the auction, he asked me if there was anything I might need in the articles listed for sale. I told him that there was just one thing – the Primus stove. I already had one of these stoves but the burner was faulty and in wartime it was quite impossible to replace it. In a house without electricity such a stove was a necessity so I told him that I would like to buy it at the sale. He explained to me that having entered it in the auction he wouldn't like to withdraw it but he said, 'You buy the stove at the auction and we'll settle the price afterwards.' That was a very generous offer.

The auction next day got under way and soon the Primus stove came under the hammer. I should point out that the price of a new Primus was eight shillings so I opened with a bid of one pound which I thought was reasonable. Right away came a bid of twenty-five shillings so I had to follow that with thirty shillings and that was how the bidding went until the opposing bid was five pounds! At this point a hush came over the crowd, perhaps they wondered if I would be daft enough to continue bidding. Well in view of the commission that I had been given I didn't hesitate very long before topping with another five shillings – making the bid what in those days would have been called five guineas!

Mementoes: Primus stove and rolling pin – antiques, but not for sale!

That finally settled the matter and the stove was knocked down to the new minister – I think I got a faint round of applause – but there were some who felt that he must either be a head-case or rolling in money! Perhaps in time they realised that he was neither!

However, the explanation to it all was very simple. The chap who bid against me was an auctioneer and one of his clients had asked him to attend the auction and to buy the Primus stove regardless of price, a commission very like my own!

That evening when the fuss was over Mr McKee and I discussed the whole business and soon we came to the matter of the Primus stove. He, of course, was entitled to the final bid of five guineas, but in his quiet manner he said. 'Would a pound be all right?' and refused to accept a penny more. That old stove did a great job in those days of austerity and, believe it or not, fifty years further on, it still works!

These two mementoes are now antiques and might be quite valuable but they are not for sale because they recall memories of two delightful people, who by their simple actions proclaimed two important qualities in Christian living – the keeping of a promise and the right attitude to money.

33

O Death, where is thy Sting?

In recent years there has been a growing tendency for Christian people to regard death not just as a time of sadness and mourning, but rather as an occasion for praise and thanksgiving for the life of the one who has 'fought a good fight, finished the course and kept the faith'. In the Christian church we have good reason for this attitude to death for Paul, knowing that at any moment he might lose his life, is able to share with us his glorious certainty, 'For me to live is Christ and to die is gain'. This experience of the indwelling Christ is available to us all and with it comes the glad assurance of victory over death.

But another trend has appeared in recent years amongst those who appear to have no belief in the truths of the Gospel. Here we note an effort being made to dispel the fear and darkness of death by introducing various kinds of bright music, light-hearted readings, often from strange sources and a eulogy that will contain a tribute to the deceased and lots of humour for the congregation! How pathetic and shallow it all is and how disappointing for those who have lost loved ones.

May I bring to you a very different scenario where premature death was faced with grace and courage and a glorious assurance of what lay beyond the grave.

First the story of Mervyn who grew up in our congregation, First Dromara, passing through Sunday School and the various youth organisations. He was especially interested in the Boys' Brigade and had the makings of a good officer and excellent leader, but it was not to be. The first signs of trouble arose on his return from the B.B. summer camp. At first it seemed that it was just the result of a cold or perhaps a virus that would soon disappear, but this did not happen and eventually his condition was diagnosed as leukaemia. Mervyn was not, of course, told how serious the disease could be but he was a thoughtful lad and soon realised that his future was somewhat uncertain.

One evening he came to the manse to discuss and to learn about the Church's ministry of healing. We talked about it for a long time and I was surprised by some of his questions, revealing a keen brain and a remarkable grasp of religious matters. He had taken his first Communion some years before this and I knew at the time that he had given it all much thought and as a result it was a very important milestone in his journey through life. So he had a good foundation on which to build and he gladly agreed to come to the manse for prayer support and ministry.

After a few visits there was a definite improvement in his condition, which of course, could be regarded as simply a period of remission, but certainly both physically and spiritually he seemed to be a different person. He even suggested that one day we might climb to the top of Slieve Donard!

I thought that was rather ambitious, but not wanting to disappoint him, agreed that we could go part of the way and a day was arranged for our assault on Donard! But before the proposed date, Mervyn had a serious set-back and was taken to hospital and there he realised just how dangerous his disease was, but he never gave up hope. Reminiscent of St Paul, he told me that there were two possibilities regarding his future; if he were to get better he had planned to become a full-time youth worker in the Presbyterian Church and if this did not happen he would be in glory with his Lord. Mervyn did not recover and his passing caused much heart-break in his family and amongst all who knew him, but what a comfort to know that death for him was not the end but the beginning of a wonderful new life. 'O death, where is thy sting?'

Our theme reminds me of another outstanding person, Norman, a young married man in his 30s whose body apparently was riddled with cancer. He had undergone many operations and a number of organs had been removed but the disease persisted. His minister, Malcolm Scott, invited me to join him on a visit to Norman who had requested this. That first visit wasn't a very happy one for Norman was in a rather rebellious mood. He just couldn't understand how a God who was supposed to be a God of love, could allow him to suffer so much. He pointed out that he had tried to live a decent respectable life and had made many sacrifices for the comfort and happiness of his wife and three little children. He had looked to a happy future but now all his plans had been shattered. Many years later, I still haven't found a satisfactory answer to this tragic situation but we were on the spot and had to help in some way. In situations like this it is sometimes hard to know when to stop praying for recovery and instead to seek inner peace for the sufferer.

Both Malcolm and I felt that he was beyond the point of no return, and decided that our task was to bring him, if possible, an experience of spiritual healing. I saw him a few times after this but Malcolm was assiduous in his ministry and did a truly remarkable job. As proof of this I refer to a little scene that took place just a few days before Norman died. Malcolm had called and they were looking over the past months of suffering, disappointment and also great blessing. Suddenly he took his minister by the hand and said, 'I wish I had the opportunity of standing before a congregation and telling them about the love of God.'

Years ago as a student reading Latin, from time to time one came across the phrase, 'Mirabile Dictu', which just means, 'wonderful in the telling'. It certainly applies to Norman's unrehearsed expression of gratitude. His body was decimated with disease but his spirit soared above it all and a few days later carried him through the valley into the presence of the Saviour whom he had come to love.

'O Grave, where is thy victory?'